HIS NAME IS NEW YORK

Mariana L. Paz

HIS NAME IS NEW YORK

Poetry & Prose

Mariana L. Paz

Dedicated to the encouragement I've received
from the people I'm surrounded by—
a testament that words, people, and places
hold as much magic as one dares to embrace.

Dear Reader,

This story is about love—in its many embodied forms—and the mirror it holds when one discovers it. For me, it came in the untangling of knots as distance pulled two people apart.

Love settled into the first five days of the year, the warmest days of my year. He and I were in a neighborhood called Arcadia, a name fitting for the state of mind we shared. I was wrapped, a falling porcelain cup thriving in its fragility.

From Texas, I waved, firmly grounded in his promises, as New York took him away. But the past likes to spread where it finds space to grow—1,500 miles stretched taut with hurt. Days became battles, and I, an injured soldier, serenading the trenches.

My anguish permeated my writing. I let it, hoping little by little it would disappear. I journaled to make sense of my insecurities, and scribbled poems became the only comfort that sustained me.

Eventually, I learned something from the words I couldn't bring myself to say—a map of prose and poetry, seamlessly intertwined. Together, they tell the story of mind and heart, person and city, love and loss—both beautiful and chaotic—at the center.

Yellow Cab Rides

The polluted air greets me
with gleams of encouragement.
Thorns in my crown of roses
urge my return to greener land.

The lives of nomadic souls
mimic unending carousel rides,
while the wanderer's mischief
irrevocably overwhelms a weak mind *like mine*.

But the danger outside my brick tower
can't be worse than the monsters I sleep with at night.

So, in the broken promises
that cloud the New York City sky,
I convince the yellow cabs
that a city as restless as theirs
could only be suitable for a spirit
as tangled as mine.

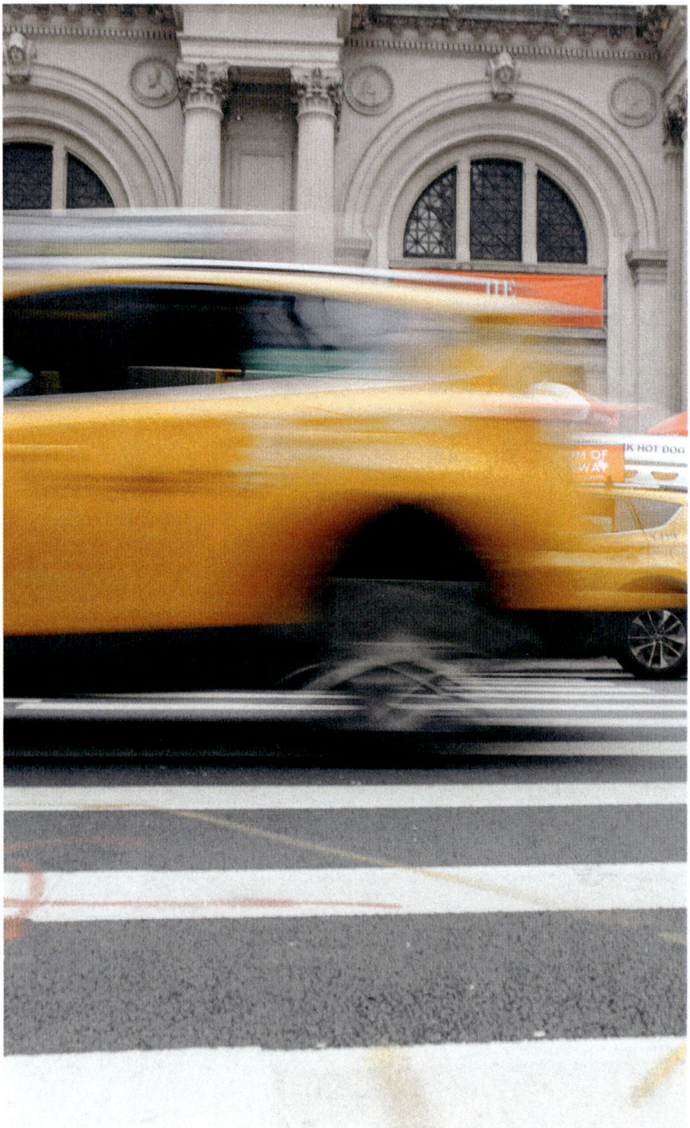
HOT DOG

The Roses' Kindness

Everyone here regards themselves kind
until their unscratched finger
meets the thorn of the first rose.
Bleeding becomes an irreconcilable act.

The cutter crowns himself a victim
defames the rose's nature as wicked.
Blame falls on the rose and curse upon the flowers.
One by one, gardens die under skyscrapers.

Everyone here regards themselves kind
until asked to smell the roses and let them by.
If beauty can't be kept for their own fulfillment
they'd rather see the rose die.

Blood will always pump, if a heart is kind
to forgive and embrace the morning sun.
The bitter become corpses before their day comes
avoiding beauty and pain at their own expense.

Everyone here regards themselves kind
clapping at the righteous' downfall like a circus spectacle.
If so, I'd rather be unkind to all and cut by a thousand thorns
than die unscratched with an empty soul.

How long will I wonder
if the love I give is the *right one*,
if it's the way it should be
or if it's the reason
people always leave?

I visited New York City for the second time. I went with the underlying thought that I could build a bridge between closure and happy endings. In an attempt at courage in the name of growth, I made peace with the joy and sadness I would encounter. However, I was naive to the proportions and moments they would be served in. Wishful thinking tends to defeat the reason in me. It's so strong that at times like these it silences the whispering intuition asking me to stop. But I believe in the benefit of the doubt. I believe the world's biggest strength is in its acts of kindness. And if I need to be vulnerable in order to prove my strength, I will gracefully accept the loss of my own mistakes. I landed on the island unsure if my steps were the result of an impulsive weakness or a virtuous conviction.

Alice

It's a hazard to listen to the voice in my head
I've got so many.

Their grim methods meddle
down the dirty hollows I curiously follow,
always tempting me to plaster pain on paper.

They mock the fragility of my flaws.
Cruelty, like a muscle, is only meant
to make my soul grow stronger.

I hear the lions roar, a sound similar
to sirens across the other door.

I hear the fairies and the birds
the kings and the pawns

the lost children
and the widowed dolls.

While the rabbit and the mouse
fill empty cups with poisoned thoughts,
all awaiting my answer:

—"The queen's gone mad!"
chasing nightmares in the name of love.

Eat me
Drink me
Choose me
Love me

A Fool's Desires

I used to ask heaven to let me live
many lives instead of one,
to have homes in many cities
and different lovers in each one.

I'd ask the stars for different wishes.
Whispers of my late father
become echoing thoughts:
—"A fool is what a fool wants."
Where my head wants freedom
my heart wants love.

I would ask heaven to let me live
beyond forever; today is fine,
to sing along to the songs of change
and turn the page when the time came.

But in every attempt to seduce the stars
I fell deeper for the ones I saw in his arms.
A fool is what a fool does.
I asked for love...
to never last this long.

Hope's Mercy

My mother prayed for love
at even times of abundance and despair.
—"His wealth is made of it and He likes to share."
Love is strength, love is kind,
love is selfless, love doesn't blind.
But I'm weak, distrusting, and hurt. I'm broke.

I gamble my cursed currencies,
hoping little by little I'll disappear.
Merciless time, shift the odds to my side
I'll book a flight to Wonderland
and in plain sight, with the insane, hide.

My father prayed to evenly share
in moments of abundance and despair.
—"It always comes back multiplied;
      if not this time... in the afterlife."
The more I give, the more I lose,
the more I wait, the more I bruise.
But I'm restless and tempestuous, stubborn, and sublime.

I gamble the chance to leave with grace
I'm at the mercy of hope.
Can a make-believe vision of love
become real to the eyes of God?

Voices say don't but I don't care anymore.
I'll take the punch, I'll take the pain,
I'll take the hell, I'll take the shame.
I've nothing left, so let the games begin.

A Tree Grows in Brooklyn

I hope my thoughts get lost
in the wrinkles of the city's buildings
and remain trapped in the spider's web.

The old couple in the park said,
—"Abundance lies in the years ahead."
I fear there isn't enough road left.

I'd drink the gas of the cabs to drive further away
taking passengers with me for however long they'd like to stay.
I'd eat the worms buried in Central Park
feeding off the spirits who never made it far.

But I'm neither a bird nor a cab.

I'm a tree growing in the middle of Brooklyn.
I grow under the pressures and stumbles of stones
more and more under the absence of light.

However many years left I get
I'm afraid I'm planted in a place,
where trees aren't meant to last.

I tried to shield my thoughts with blinders. Tried to force myself to see only what optimism teaches me, in other words: gaslight my heart into happiness. A part of me was submerged in a blissful sea. The city has a way of turning sadness into magic, dirt into dusty particles of inspiration, and vandalism is simply art. Unfortunately, my thoughts found a way out and wandered off to the innermost corners of my mind; painting the city in beautiful shades of blue. Similar to when I was a little girl, rather than play outside in the welcoming sun, I'd barge into my mother's closet to dust off old memory boxes. I'd look at old pictures from my parents' wedding. They seemed happy. I'd fantasize about those days; before the divorce washed the fairy tale away. Eventually, I saw the pictures for what they were: evidence of broken promises. I became nostalgic for a past that never happened, for a present that isn't there, and a future that could've been. Before, nostalgia only visited my door through cigarette scents, memory boxes, and old rock songs. Now it was everywhere. I remain still like a photograph that hasn't been properly revealed, paralyzed in the smile. In that split second, I understood the present no longer existed; it was gone.

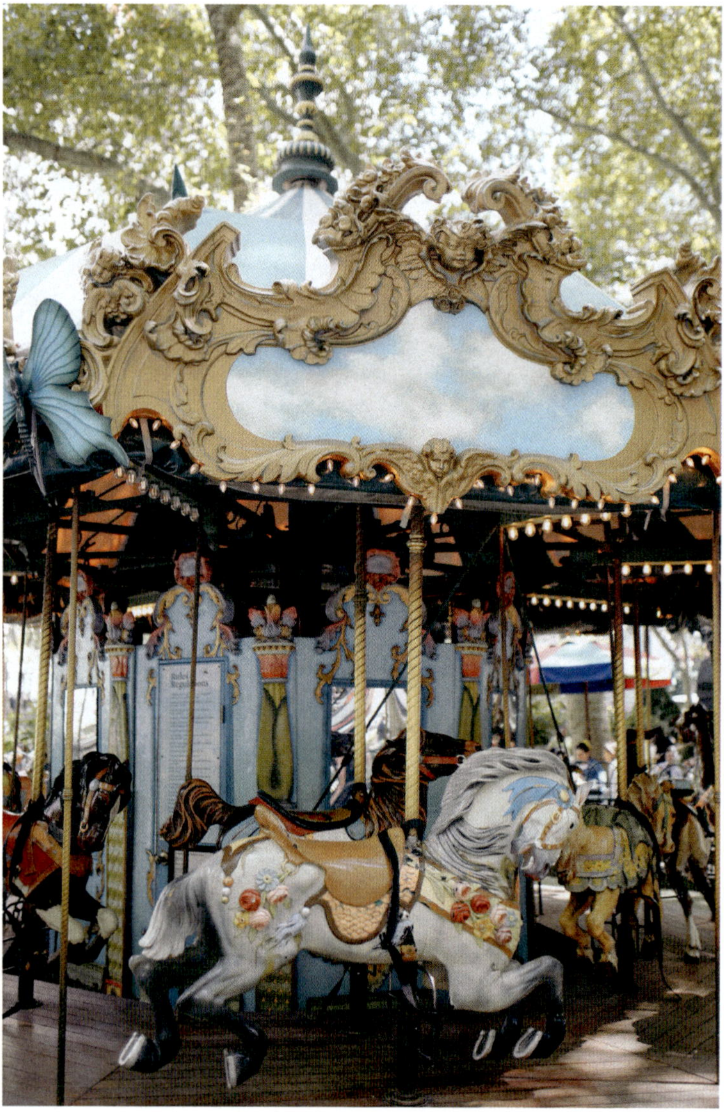

Flying Horses

There was a time in my life
I was nothing more and nothing less than happy.

I would run around and pick up on things
a child shouldn't give much thought about.

I wondered, "Is it normal for the husband to not kiss the wife?"
or "Is it normal for the wife to sleep in the daughter's bed at night?"
I didn't mind. My concern was focused on why horses couldn't fly.

But then a time came
when half the drawers and hangers lost purpose
and the bed was half empty on Saturday mornings.

That was the day I stopped caring
if behind the clouds, danced flying horses.

Arcadia

Arcadia is a place...
behind the riverbends
where my father hides.
In the minute after midnight
when magic stays with those she likes.

A place under the bedsheets
where time stops and souls
collide when our hands touch.
In the agonizing pleasures felt only in shared silence.

A place where the blind see
over the faraway hills
at the edge of madness.
In between the fragments of unboxed memories.

A place were peace
above the stars
comes at no cost.
In the stories that weren't meant to end
or can't be measured in linear time frames.

Arcadia exists...
in the second before the first tear sheds
and a sigh of relief meets the first breath of grief.
There I'll rest.

Circa 98

How many years have I remained still
waiting for heaven to knock?

                                              I saw an angel once
                                   it was a man promising love.

An Instance's Lock

In make-believe skies
underneath different stars
I envy the girl who sleeps in your arms.

The strangers on the subway or elevator stop
who get to see your face
and share an instance of your day.

My fairy tales turn to dust
I burn my present longing for "should've"
of what is not.

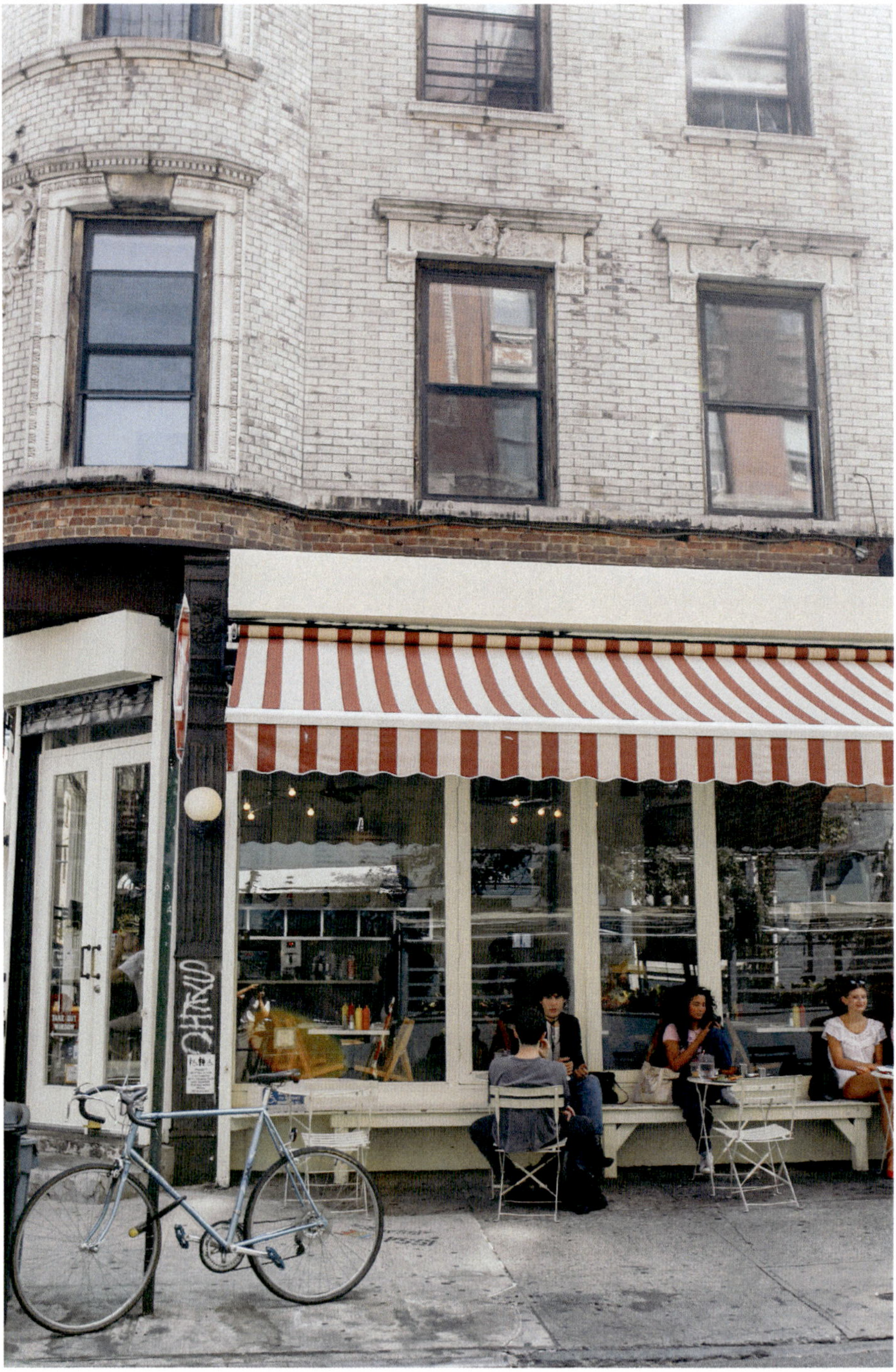

Midnight Travels

The passing of time has me wishing
I had more hours at night.
I see clearest in the absence of light.
The sun becomes a camera flashing
forcing me to smile for those around.

    But when everyone sleeps
    I am finally free.
    I roam around the different cities
    my soul once lived in.
    10 p.m.
        11 p.m.
            Midnight
                1 a.m.
                    2 a.m.
                        3 a.m.
                            Four...
                            I went to Paris in 1974.
                            It wasn't Texas or New York
                            but there you were.
                            I wrote a poem; you sang a song.

NEW YORK & HIM

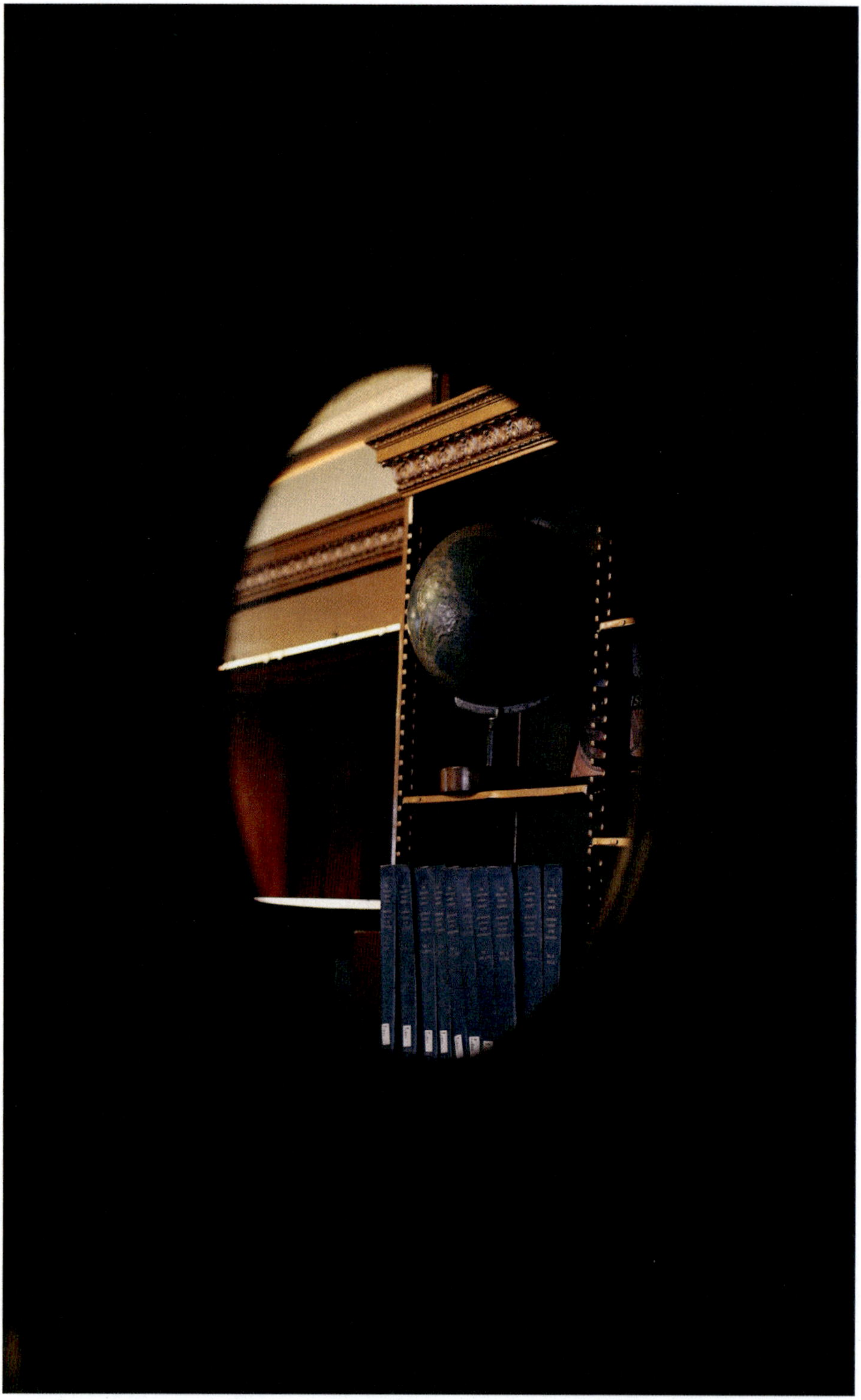

In the Name of

Addictive tendencies are my religion
the holy trinity of self-loathing.

There's nostalgia in *nicotine* smoke;
in my late grandfather's libraries
in the armchair where I fell in love with books
and the Christmas parties
whose joy got lost
in a closeted memory box.
My cynical fascination for exhaling poison
dares the years ahead, purposefully disregarding death.

There's laziness in *caffeinated* drinks.
They're easy, sustenance's low road
shortcuts to other drugs in human form.
Pours of accomplishment
served with the slightest effort.
I dare the dreams ahead; I'll rest when I'm dead.

Then there's *love*,
four letters parallel pain.
Doesn't need ornaments around it
to stand at the center of the world's maleficence.
My only witness to prove the world has magic,
a divine alchemy
between witchcraft and God,
beyond terrestrial, beneath celestial.
Misfortune's checkmate.

I live in the space between "in" and "sanity,"
searching for it.

I have a soft spot for the magnificent city of New York and the person that now lives in it. I can't explain the reasons behind my deeply rooted affection for either. Yet, their entrance into my life felt like a flood of rain, after previous years of inevitable grief condemned me to an endless drought of hope and affection. I met in both a strange sensation of comfort only found in recognition. In this person, I found safety to explore myself and acceptance within my flaws. I knew him from a memory of a past life; just like I recognized this city as home from some other time. To be loved is to be seen, and in their eyes, I again saw *me*.

Stray Dog

Roaming the crowded streets
the clouds above the floating heads all seem empty.
There's nothing kind in them to think
soft voices go unheard; endearment is never loud when true.

A stray dog sobs, it once found joy in arms called home
until the rats ate the arms and seized the core's vault.
Integrity was corrupted and the crumbs left, tarnished.

Everyone lives in the future of the next minute, hour, station.
Empty streets thirst for words only a heart of gold can speak
to drink the nectarine that pours from our eyes when they meet.

The stray dog digs a piece of heaven in concrete ignorance
bursting cries in agonizing silence, filing its claws to shreds.
But he resists the urge to feast the rats
blood and pain cannot persist when love like ours exists.

I love the same way the stray dog reeks
it penetrates the senses and suffocates the weak.
Not everyone has the heart to love
a broken animal whose core remains untouched.

Graceful Surrender

I used to envy
the graceful fall
of the autumn leaves;
now their surrender
only makes me sad.

You've been on my mind
since that November night
now I understand,
you lived there long before—

before my joy got tossed
through the seasons
before the heartbreak
of our teenage years
before the pressures
of mad men instigated fear
before the beatings
by perpetrators I held dear.

We met one another
when embracing uncertainty
was the cost of living
 not the price of bravery.

And when your eyes
found themselves in mine
I knew autumn
was once a season
that made me glad.

Sedentary Hypocrisy

I remember
the time travels
of my nights paused
for momentary conversations
with him.

The fascinating memories
of my journeys dissolve
but never how in his voice
I wish to remain stationed.

Thank you, Clowns

There's hands, places, and songs
whose frost mends open scars.

There's hearts, papers, and sheets
whose madness guards your sanity.

There's clowns, poets, and gamblers
whose misfortune impels your wealth.

There's cities, people, and years
whose presence turns you timeless.

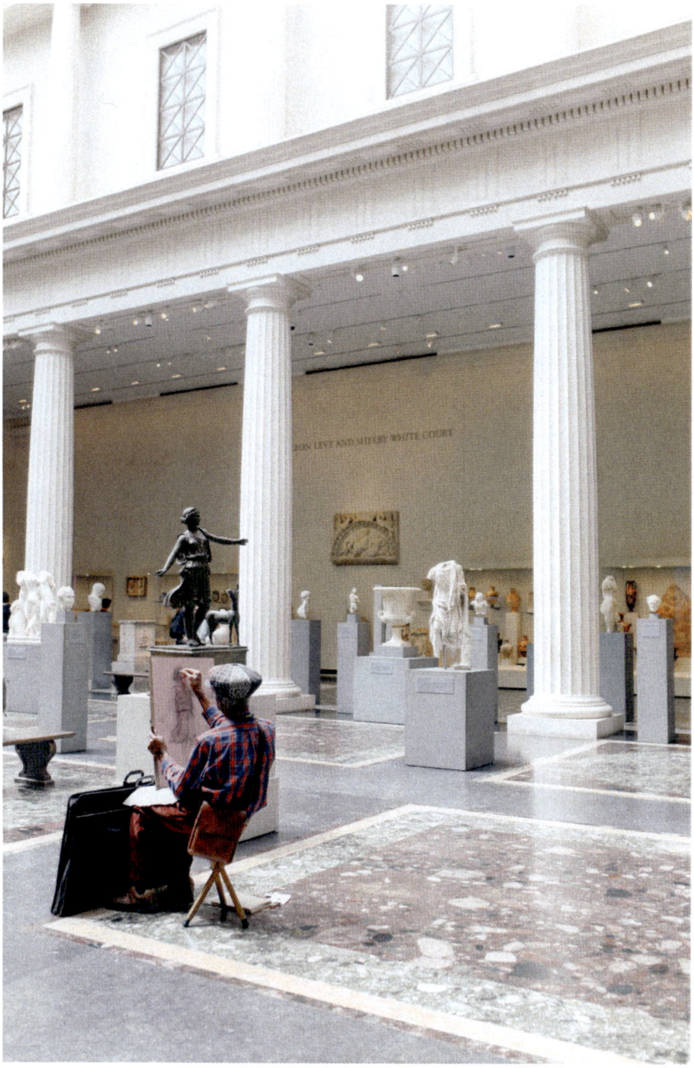
WHITE COURT

The Butterfly

She slides into conversations that don't concern her
unwitnessed
unnoticed
unworthy of consideration
for her lack of blush.

Never like the glorified butterfly
who strikes conversations
as she incites new ones.

I never heard the crowd praise,
"Look at the beautiful butterfly,"
when I stepped on stage.

—"But a butterfly is a butterfly
even when her wings are tinted gray,"
you said.

The first time I walked around the city, I was immediately struck by its magnificence. Its archaic infrastructure blends effortlessly with the relevance of modern times. The way the old remains a basis for the new. The people it has touched, the conversations it has witnessed, the inspiration it brought to the artists it birthed. No particular trait is essential to explain its incandescent beauty. It simply, as a whole, is wonderful. It's a city whose spirit calls for me to stay despite no obvious indication of it. No job offers, no relatives, no friends, only a mutual understanding that we both have a deep desire to share a period of our lives with one another.

When desire and recognition meet
uncertainty shakes hands with peace.

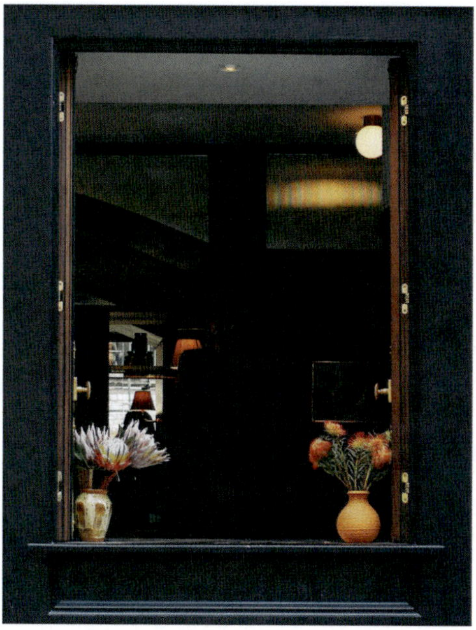

Paper Veil

It feels silly to dedicate
a love letter to someone
who receives one each day
a letter, a song, a curse.

I see him stand.
His indifferent cool
paralyzes my spine.
So oblivious
to the sentiments he evokes,
forcefully naive
to the moments
his name
crosses my mind.

I see him stand and wonder,
—"How will the roses smell...
if someday we collide and
roam the same realms?"

A smile, a tear, a year.
At the edge of his core
relying on madness
to sustain our joy,
peacefully drowning
in earth's decadence.

I love him.
If he calls I'll go
an intrusive angel tells me
it's safe to do so.

Band-aid Arms

His eyes wrap a blanket around me
healing bruises with every stare.

His gaze lifts up my world
after it crumbled with the wrong words.

Patching with band-aids the castle walls
he urges the pawns to return home.

—"The queen has found love!"

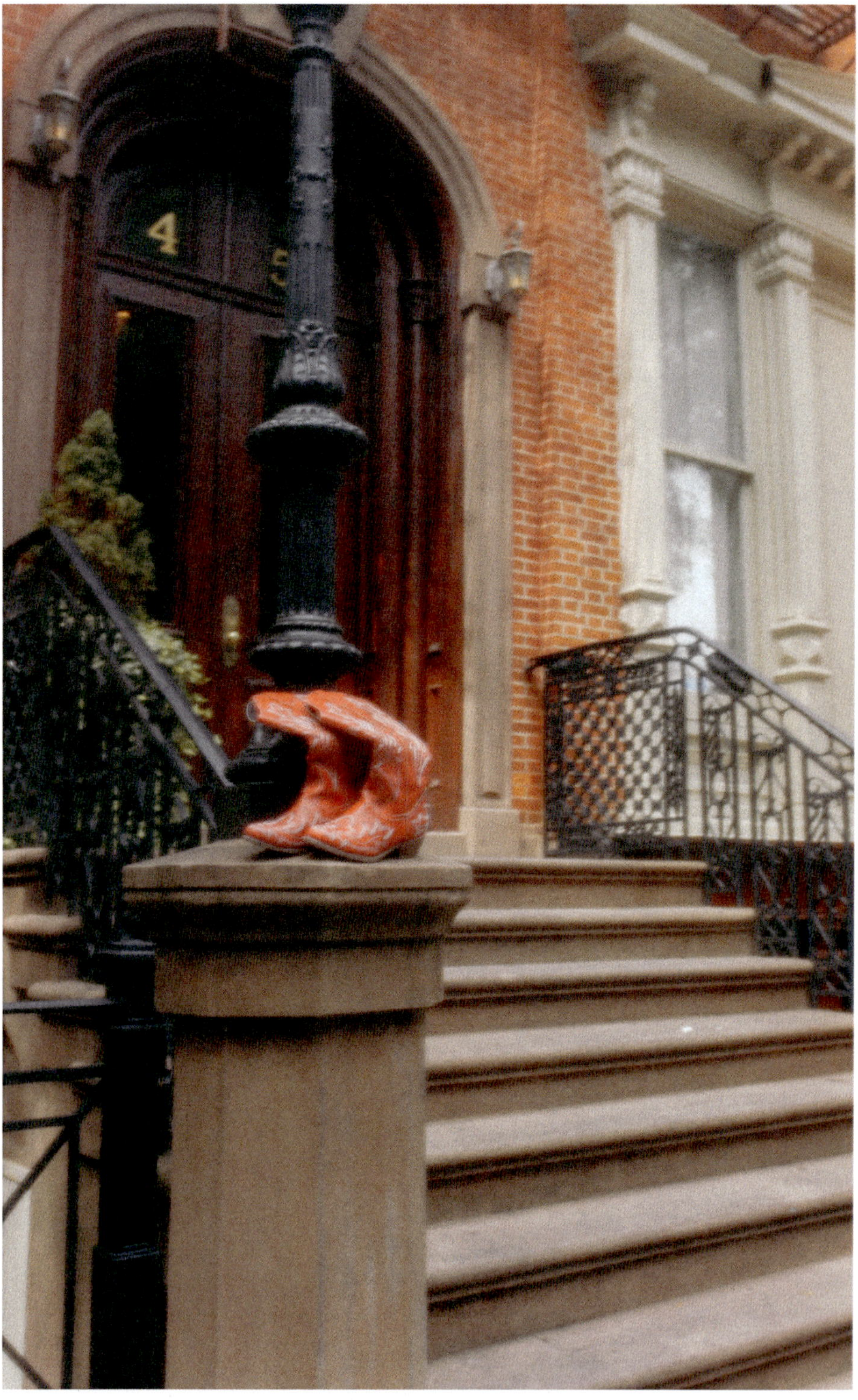
4

Cookeville, TN

Is there a place we can meet?
Between your roaring city
and my Texas streets?

Away from selfish sidewalks
and tangled six-lane highways,
spreading urban greed
over self-made gardens.

Far from this so-called home
we can call our own?
Where your silence
meets my loudness
and in our madness
my world becomes yours.

I'll suppress my yearn for Spanish
if literature is all you can offer.
You'll no longer need to wander
at home, you'll never be lost.

A home where midnight
brings you daylight
a place where our souls can speak,
in a language I create for you
in stories you read to me.

Amputee

A piece of me
is devoted entirely to you.
I can't contain it
but I'm tempted to break apart
and limp around from year to year.
All it takes is one word
to propel the spread
and all of me will belong
to *only* a piece of you.

Mystical Lover

Tell me if sparks fly from our encountered eyes
or if you read my mind when your skin kisses mine.
Tell me how your serenity combs my fears
and heals my porcelain cracks like a Japanese artisan.

Our story has been told by many folk singers before.
It sketched the mountains to find our way through different roads.
The stumbles and headaches we perished tied a knot
so we'd always be together even when apart.

Like puppets, we sang for operas.
I performed for the whims of lovers— annointed *martyrs*
who tore and tossed my light into a million stars
... all in the name of "God" or perhaps "love."
Ships wrecked, but only you traced constellations with my scars.

So tell me if I'm the moon your ocean tides dance to
for you're the sun my heavens welcome
when the rooster sings your name.
Will mystical sparks burn our love to ash
or can they ignite the bonfire that lets the winter pass?

Baby, I have a compass that only points North
and you can find me South when New York gets cold.
Time is all we've got if we agree on the time and place
we'll someday fall in love.

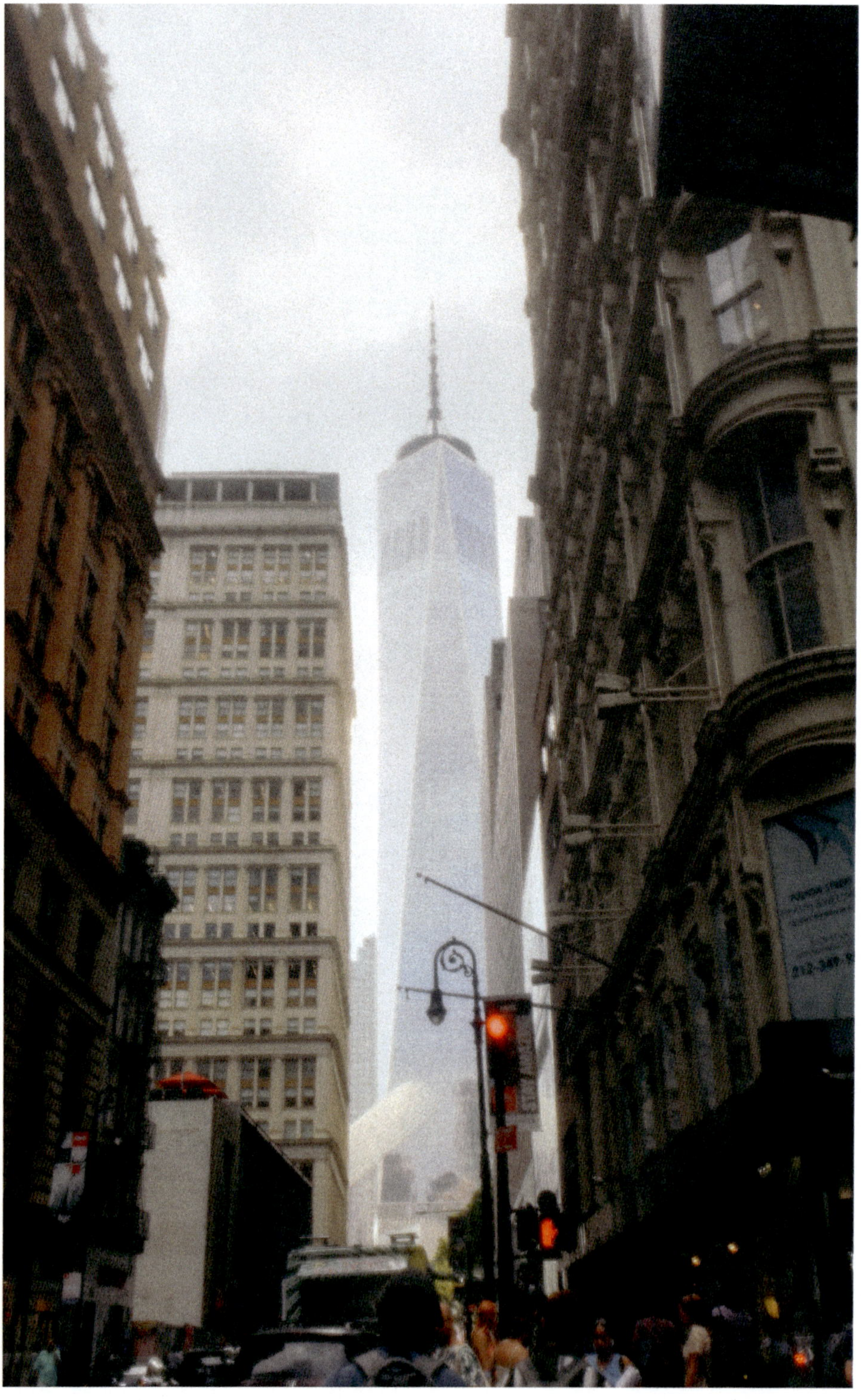

In those same words I could vaguely express the feelings I've always had for this person. A stranger's presence was a heart-warming invitation to peace. A sentiment I was subconsciously longing to experience found me in the shape of this man. In just one night, he entered my home, poured some coffee, and decided to indefinitely stay. And without any physical indication of it, I heard a call to do the same.

My affection for him morphed into something greater than I ever imagined it could. I saw this connection as a once-every-so-often coincidence, unintetionally bumping into each other from time to time. Living mostly in a make-believe reality that he might share the same sentiments as I. A platonic relationship, the kind I only found in movies and books. Not possessive, or apprehensive, with no expectations that kill the joy of every relationship. However, our invisible string pulled harder this time and left us face to face with a choice. A decision to become present in each other's life in more than just mind or soul. A promise to join our days and thoughts, to create our own world in which to live by. It looked beautiful.

To Live in Your Kintsugi

I fall asleep with visions of your mind.

I dream of the daily crimes it commits
protected by the silence it exudes.

The intruder to your intrusive thoughts
prays to sit by the wanderings behind your smirk.

And share thrilling pieces of daily assassinations
of the villains we see on subway stations.

Fulfill my wish to get lost in your kintsugi lines
and memorize the childhood hauntings you wish to erase.

At the very least keep them safe, so their torment
won't rain over today's wicked child's play.

Astrology in Love

His sun was in Leo;
it aligned with my stars.
I saw him from afar in a crowded place
and the town turned quiet.
Dreadfully beautiful
when he remembered
my name.
I was blinded by clarity
willingly surrendered to the force in his eyes.
I make love to them when I close mine.
My moon was in Cancer;
but it now found its sun.

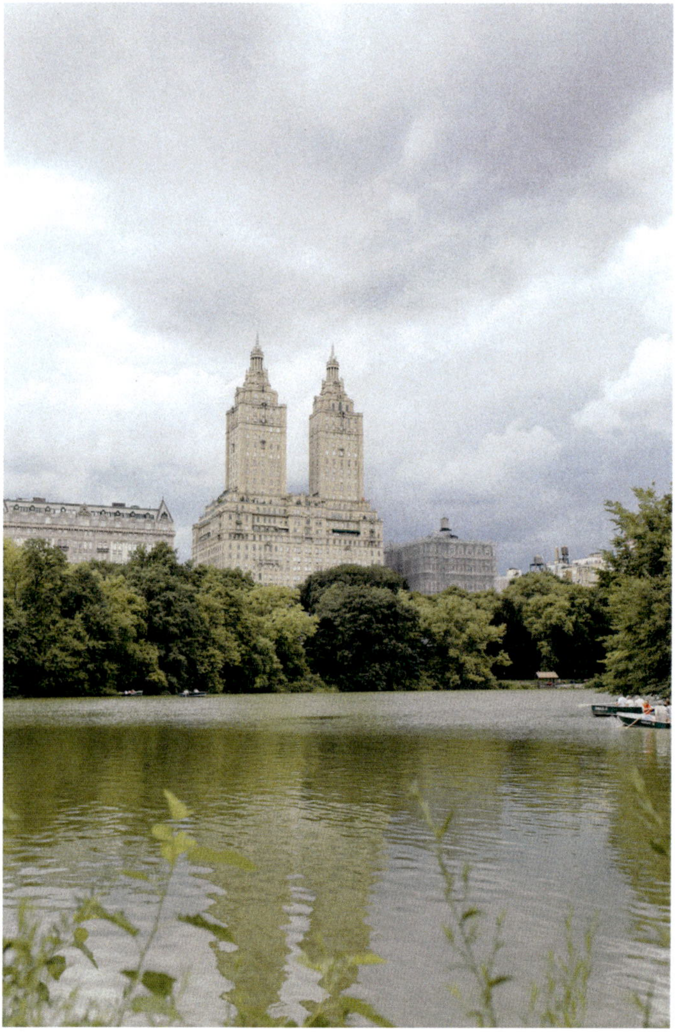

November 26, 1975

If my sobriety saw the vividness
I see with whiskey nights...

I'd say it was 1974 or the winter of '75
when the walks around the park
were for the free and homeless,
like equals they roamed
while the rats hid from the glimmers of hope.

—"Are you homeless or broke?" I asked.
—"I'm a romantic... guess that makes me both."
—"Can you light my cigarette? I'm cold."

I saw corpses in the naked trees
but you saw beauty in their clarity.

And from that winter to the next
I remembered... it's for you
I no longer dread December.

Liquor Devour Me

Step into the gardens of Babylon with me
walk my steps and guard your breath.

Let our whispering thoughts
like tickles stimulate your lungs.

Carry me to heaven
through the starry night your mind wears.

Baby, I pray you crown me
the guardian of your divine stairwell.

Curse my name into a song
that spells conjuring colors to paint the sky red.

Pick my flowers and drink my wine
wreck the walls of the made-up castle in my mind.

Talk to me in poetry and frame my mind with lies;
I promise I'll cry to God, so you can hear me laugh.

Keep as an oath the self-reflecting mirror in my dorm
inhale the venom off my lips that stains your mouth with gold.

Let's share the promise of forever that will only last today
and take to our grave the reminiscence
a piece of heaven got to see the human light of day.

I try not to let my world revolve around him
but his essence impregnates my skin.

His Name

He stood as an American flag waves
unbothered by squirms of men,
surrounded by smoke
like clouds of my bluest skies.

To trust him is to trust me.
In his eyes, I live.
In his jumps, I fly.
In his arms, I'm lifted.
In his dreams, mine come to life.

The alchemist of my deepest desires
peels my charades like a tangerine.

I sing his words like an anthem—
in his freedom, I am captured.

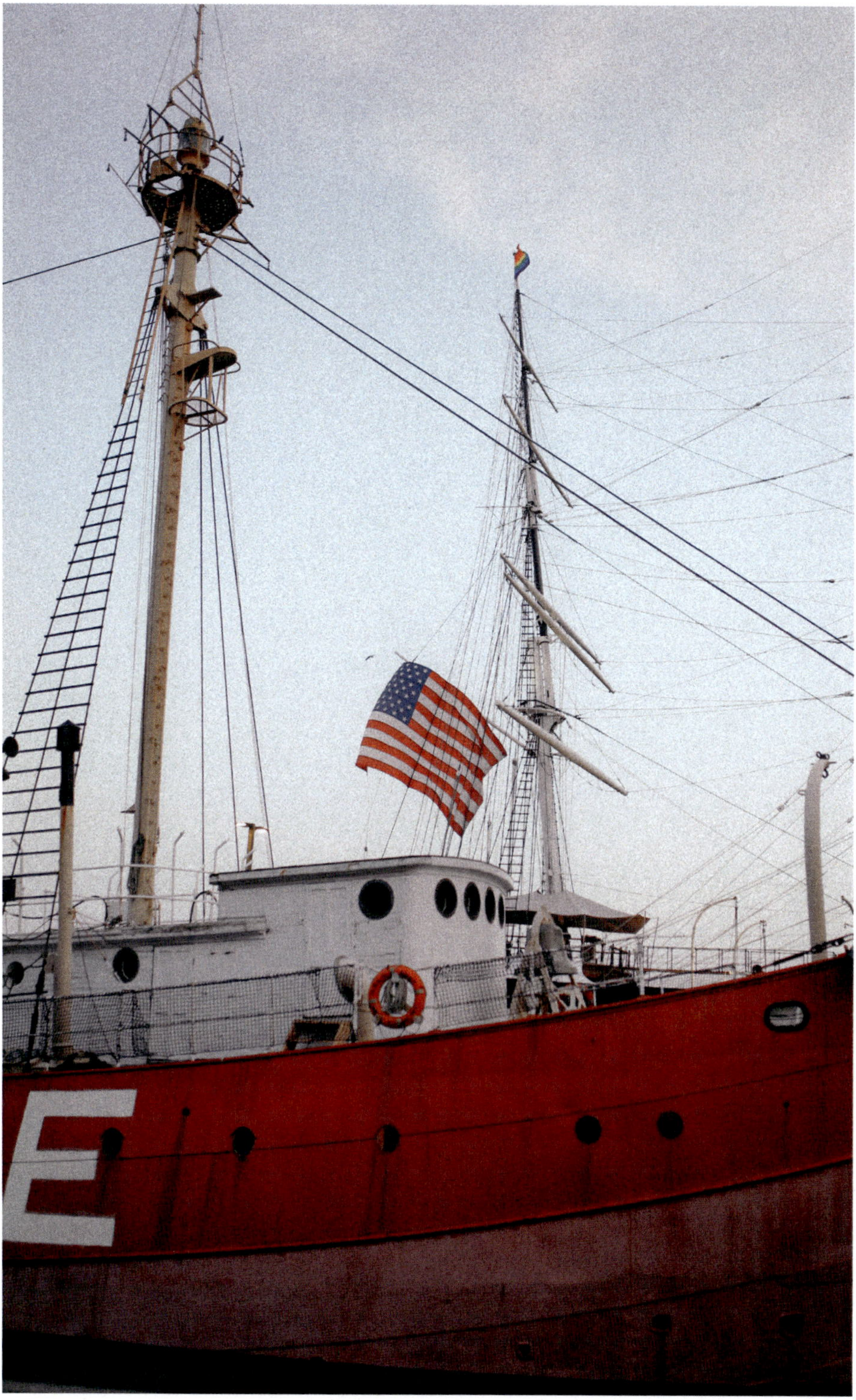

Let me carry the burdens you pray to forget.
Let me love and treasure the parts you hate.
Let the love I feel overcome the pain you once felt.

Shades of Blue

Your crimes result in my rhymes
inspiring words everywhere I go.
Reading messages while I hear your voice
becomes my favorite song.

Stars shine in broad daylight; the sun is no longer selfish.
Your gaze turns my blue skies red.
Erasing stone-carved scars like chalk on the sidewalk
your white t-shirt waves my fights away.

You've claimed real estate of mind I wasn't prepared to give.
Blue becomes my favorite color, despite its mournful shades.
Tease me like a children's book is read;
my A's of cards are no longer a secret.

All I can do is practice how my tears will wave
if one day you decide I'm not enough of anything.
I'll be left with a map of the world before there was you
for my heart, mind, and art are now yours.

If I could write...

If I ever amount to nothing
I'll always make sure you have something.

If ever I amount to something
you'll live forever in the lines I bleed.

You inadvertently entered my door
through the knock of New Year's Day.

You brought forth glimmers in dusty rooms
vividness in drunkenness
and clarity with foggy smoke.

Your peace of mind builds a bridge
in the confined torments of a tower
where I only saw walls.

Pour me some coffee while I light up your cigarette.
Please stay.

Silence is Nice

My mouth respects your presence
and admires your company's silence.

That selfless serenity
I can only find in you
is enough to fall in love
with the sentiments shared
in our unspoken thoughts.

Tiny Dancer

I swirl below the disco ball of some Tribeca bar.
Capture it

Our song plays so I dance with Hendrix and James.
Just for you

The music stops, but the guitar cries, begs to be played.
Touched

Loved
By a child whose hands aren't tied.

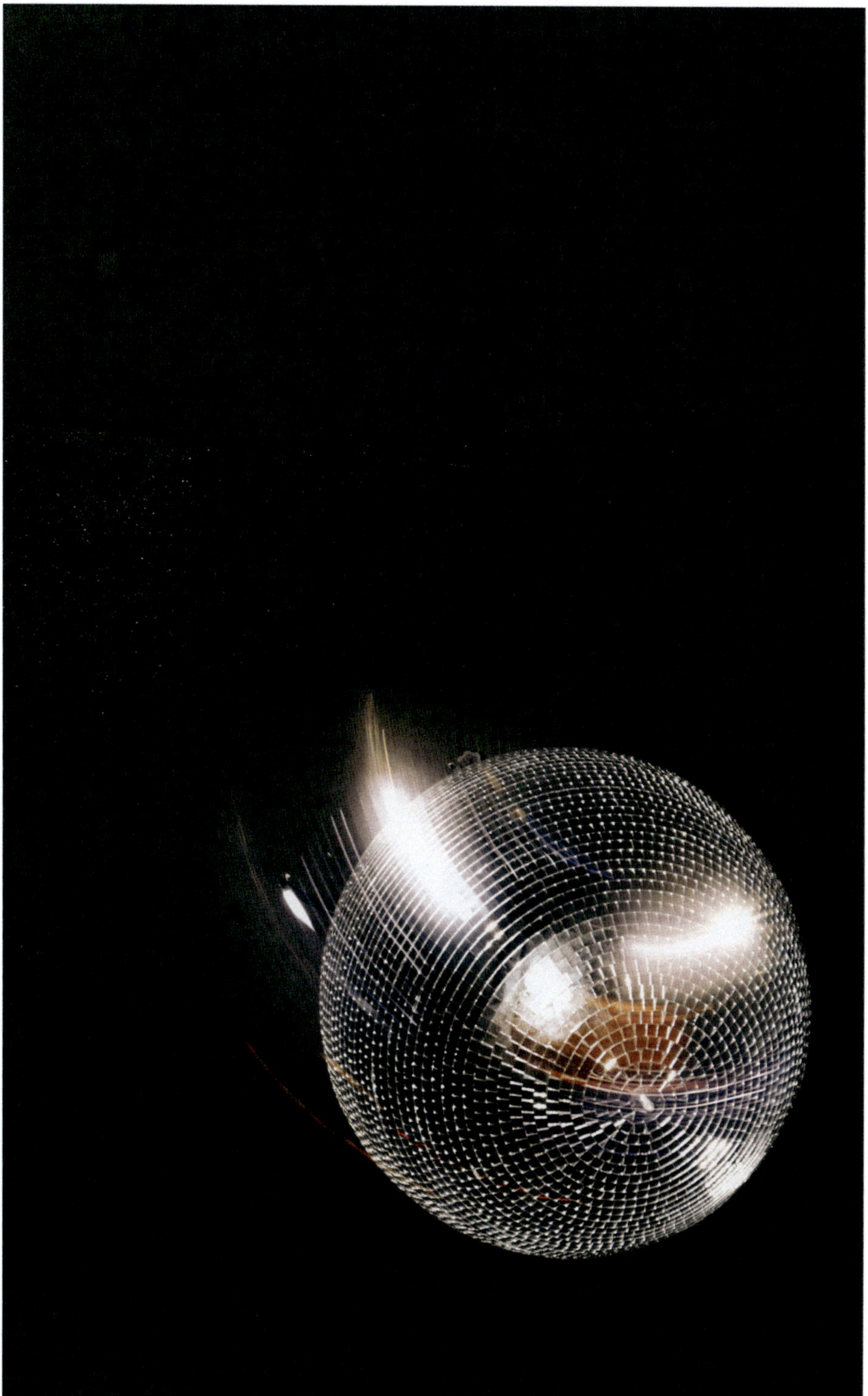

—"Your words are the only language I wish to know,
your voice is the only song I wish to hear."

That was the moment
I fell for you too,
my dear.

Crownless Beauty

You stayed
when the rabbit ran.
No point chasing time
when it comes in roses.

I was finally seen
as I imagined myself to be.
A face that only embellishes the mind
a crown to a head that by itself shines.

The heart doesn't age
when it's put to use.
The arms of my clock
will stay open for New York.

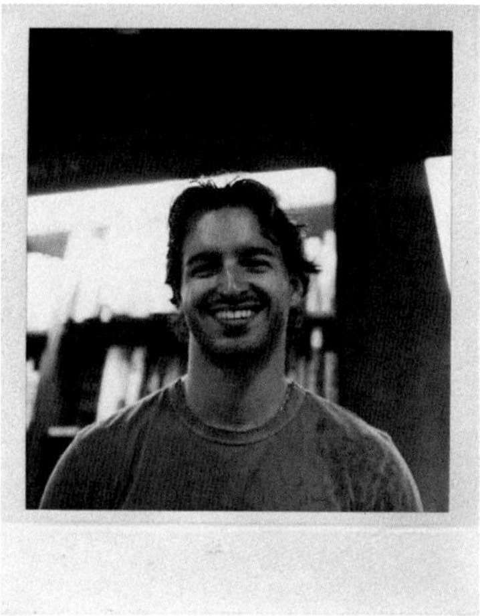

My Blind Boy

A polaroid lost in time
someone someday
behind my intentional modesty, will find.

When your presence overtakes my mouth
and I'm still.

Together, thunder wasn't loud
it was a baby's lullaby we listened to in bed.

If only I could harness the sentiments inside
we'd put New York City streets to rest.

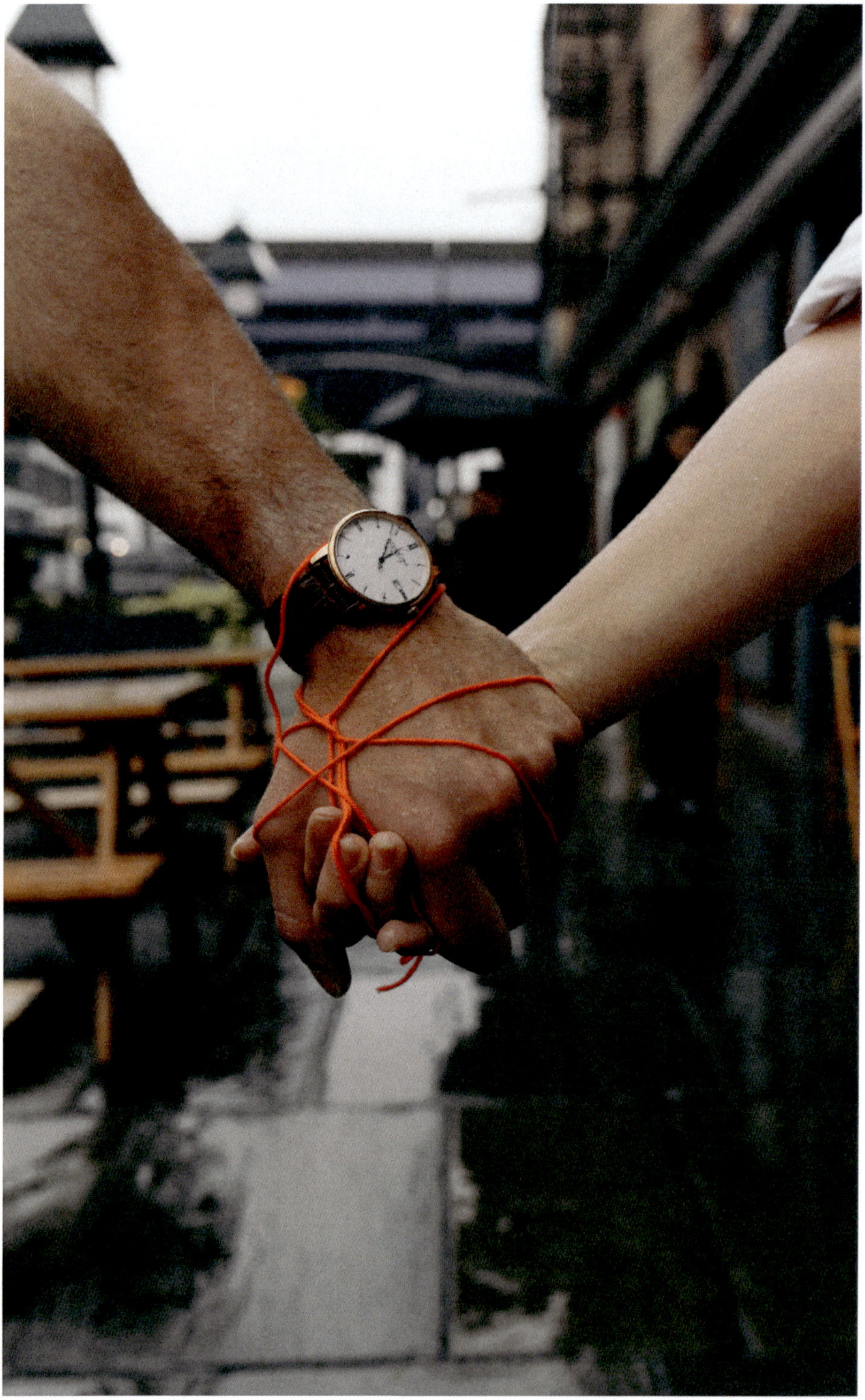

Lovers of Each Other

Could it be possible to remain lovers
from this year to the next?
From the next to the following
and ten more after that?

Lovers of the Mind, Lovers of the Art
Lovers of the Other, Lovers from Afar

Lovers
of reckless spirits in the grits of streets
of transcending novels that die unseen
of ivy wrapped in a present
that refuses to become past.

Let's live in decks of cards
witness the rise and fall
of coward rapacity.
An ongoing detriment
in the continous barks of different dogs
and emerald rusting cavity.

Could it be possible to remain lovers
live in the strokes of paintings
morphing bodies of one lover to the next.

My Downrise

Beauty lies in the eyes of the beholder
but you Are, Were, and Will Be
objectively wonderful.

Your face is a minuscule reflection
of the mind it hides
behind those saddening eyes.

For better or for worse
I'm trapped in them
constantly falling through their looking glass.

I unlearn my world to navigate yours.
Poor me, your unequivocal birthright
is the loss of mine.

Hoaxes I'll Believe

Tell me the sky is gray
and I'll learn to dance to the beat of thunder.

Tell me the fire nurtures
and watch me bloom, from the ashes a wildflower grew.

Tell me the sea doesn't drown
and I'll learn to breathe in suffocating depths.

Tell me heaven pours its pain in rays of sun
and I'll make my arms a shade for you to lie.

My soul believes the hoaxes you bleed
your mouth has no spells to cast— love is all it speaks.

In Love with Your Self

It doesn't make sense to anyone
but you and me.

A picture book no one has to read
braiding similarities
like you and I were meant to be.

Selfish stubbornness
selfless admiration
infatuated with the other's self-absorption.

Makes me wonder if you like the way I look
or if it's only the way I look at *you*.

But who cares if in darkness
he's all I see.

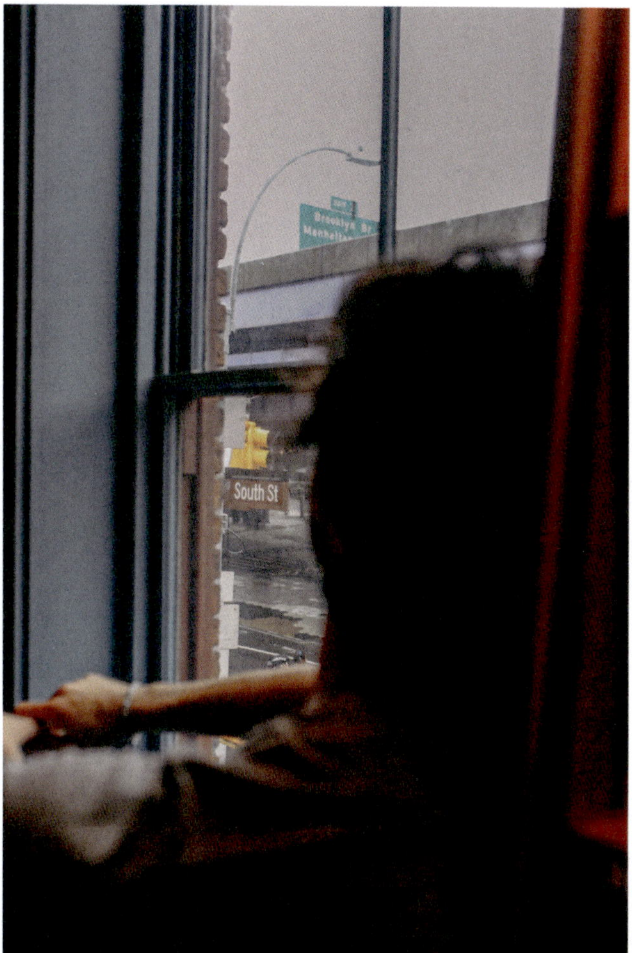
South St

Covered in New York

I find myself reading
your favorite book
playing the song you sent
a couple of nights before
with the green bookmark
from the corner vintage store.

I'm all covered in you
while you
are all covered
in New York.

Read the Lines

Never underestimate
my heart's ability to love you,
to dedicate pieces of my everyday
words, thoughts, and smiles
in your name.

If clouds of doubt haunt your mind
find shelter in my unguarded papers—
there's a message between the lines.

I'll mail them...
if you'd like.

Roaring Beats

He struck from my turbulent past
every particle of sensibility left
no one was ever able to shake.

I was electric, he was magnetic—
eclectic, an unreal presence
in the shape of him.

Suddenly I'm trapped. Framed.
A painting of surreal escapism
drowning in enlightening brush strokes.

Every step closer my beat surrenders
to match his drumming thunder.
I'm no longer mine.
I'm his—
a part of me
is.

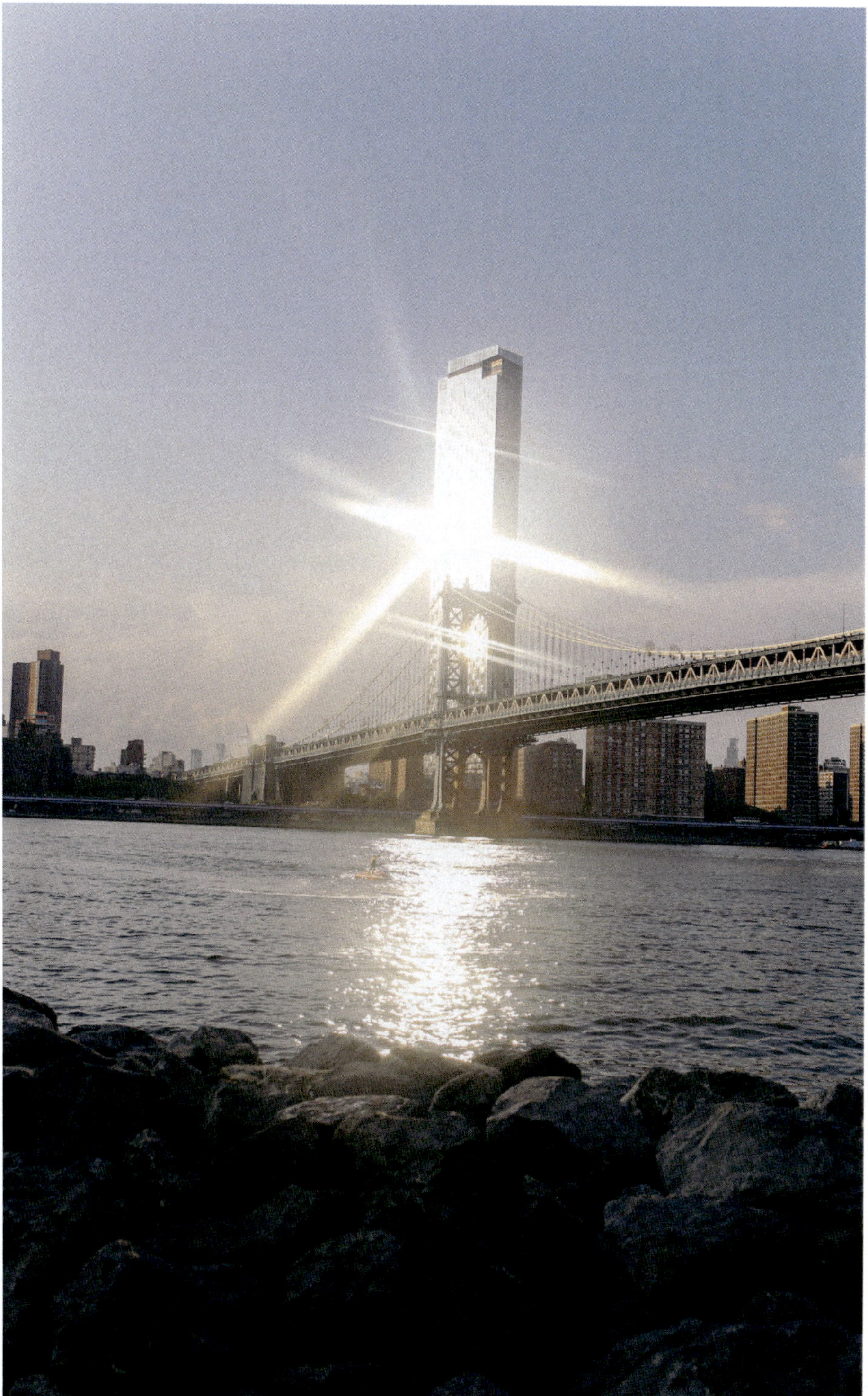

WHERE'S THE BLAME?

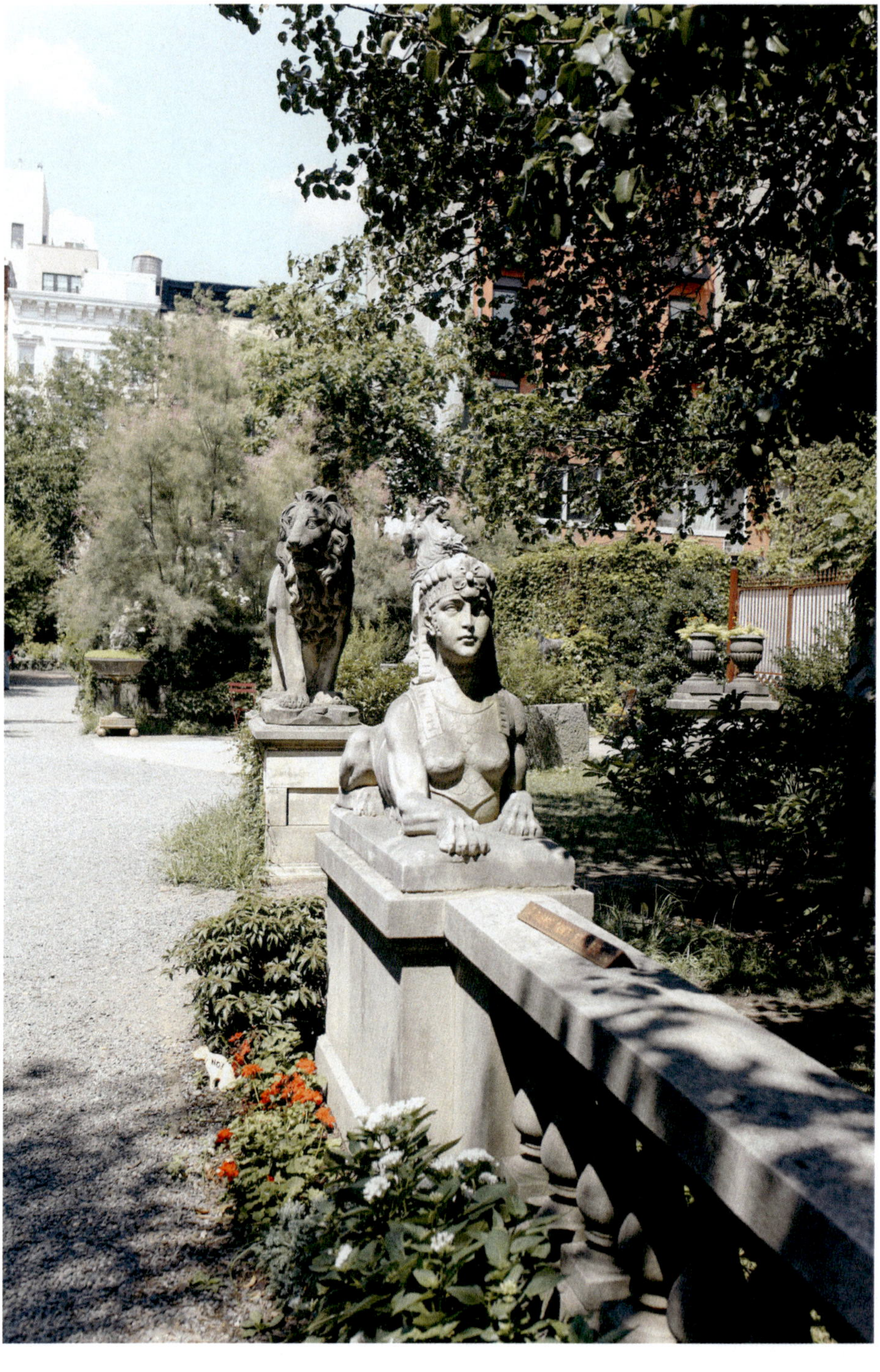

Home in the City

Lock up the damsels
parade the queens.
Push the angels; they'll fly
if they have wings.

Hunt the witches
unfit to mother
so art, poetry, and love
are all they'll have left
to wallow.

Enough to drive them mad
if lucky...
insane and hollow.

Fill the castle with portraits
of make-believe fairies
to remind them of a heaven
they'll never attain.

If lucky...
fresh new sculptures
for the asylum gates.

Once Upon a Night

There was a man who said my blues were burdens.
He couldn't bear the sight of pain.
Like a child begs, I prayed he'd stay.
Like a father loves, he left.

I was a rolling stone drowning in a pond
arousing waves in the still of time,
on a quest to test the depths of sorrow.

But when your light shrunk the darkness
my spirit remembered how to rise—
no longer hidden
no longer paralyzed.

There was a man who said my blues weren't poetry.
I wrote in secrecy until you saw the beauty in them.
My poems; your nightstand light.

You didn't care for the weight in the pages
as long as we lived the present,
your shoulder would be there
for my heart to rest.

Every fall is a chance to fly
a scared widow falling in love for the first time,
whose lover found his eyes
in mine.

First Day of the Year

You said, "I'm falling in love with you"
my fearful eyes awaken again.
Our magical connection
suddenly has an expiration date.

I'm the Old Guitar

I re-read the story, stumble on the same page.
I hear a knock from guests I don't expect.

I tiptoe at dawn, so I don't wake you up
silencing my words, so they don't reach your thoughts.

Suddenly, panic pounds my chest too strong
when I say I love you, all I think is stop.

Wish my mouth would listen and my eyes could talk
hope the distance doesn't last this long.

I try to learn new instruments, try to reach your heart
cover my scarred fingers so you don't think it's hard.
But all I know is how to play an old guitar.

I'm walking down a tightrope but the string was cut.
Convince myself that "bite the bullet" doesn't mean give up.

Wonder if I burden those I love?

Lingering echoes resemble shadows at dawn.
When I think I miss you, all I say is stop.

Wish your mind could listen to my intrusive thoughts.
Wish the distance were to blame for keeping us apart.

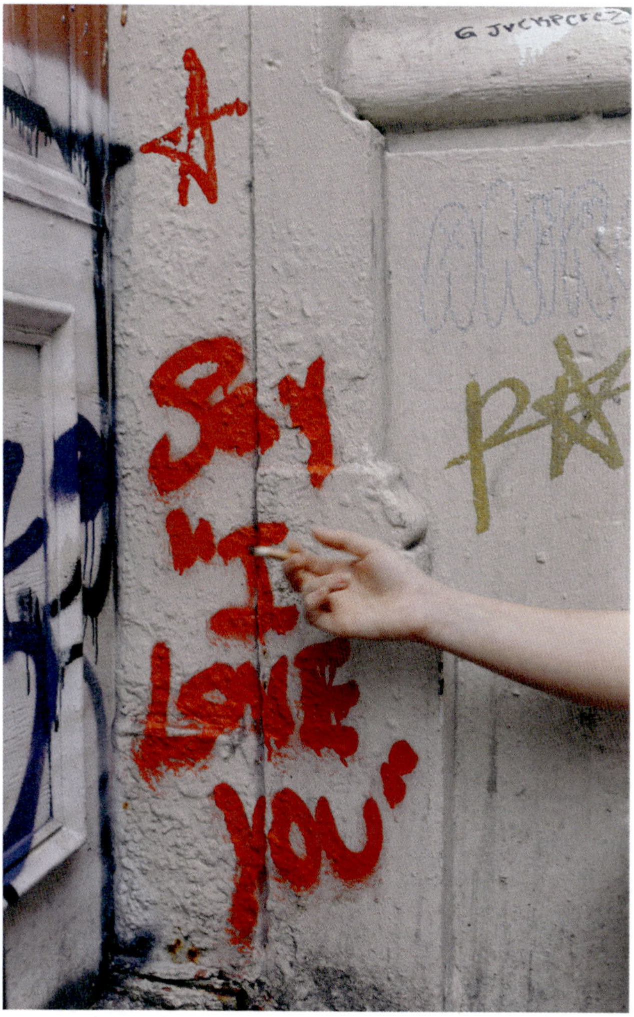
Say I love you

Cowardly loves promise "forever"
thinking "today."

The promise to fall in love and explore happiness through different fonts became a living nightmare. I once learned to fly through another man's words, but it's called falling for a reason. So, I crashed, and with me, my perception of love and identity. I thought that version of myself was buried in the pages of my past. A stone I'd visit once in a while to find inspiration for my writing and guidance for my actions. I stood corrected; she never fully died. She was petrified and opened her eyes with the breath of romantic love.

She stood up and would overtake my mind. I would see myself write things that weren't mine. I would shed tears born from irrational fears that should no longer have relevance in my life. Old scars would hurt like the day they were first cut and bleed purple blood. Scars that still had poison were rotting me from the inside out. Her voice became louder than mine and her hurts interfered with my joys. Her anxiety overshadowed my happiness and suddenly I couldn't distinguish between my past and present self anymore. We were the same, needed the same, and I felt as lost as I did the day she was born.

Free Bird

—"Fly away little bird...
                 ... go catch your dreams"

                       said a man who caged me
                       while he pushed me
                       knowing
                       I had no wings.

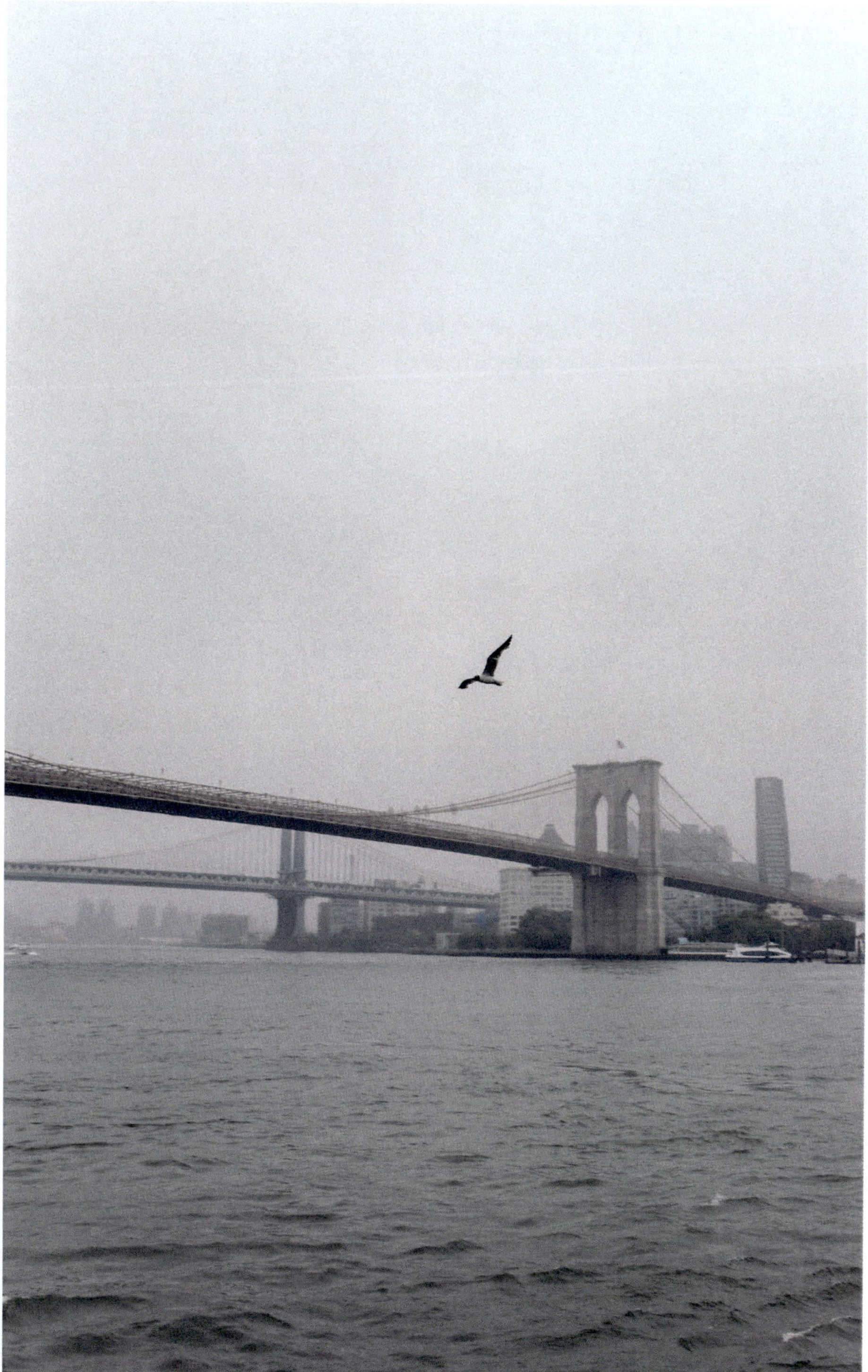

A Single Mother Locked in a Tower

I am a pregnant mother in a city of neglectful fathers.
Before the screen showed me a black-and-white vision
I already dreamed of him in full color.

My body morphs while my womb creates life; I bear magic inside.
I'm not sure when my child will breed
or when he will decide to leave,
when he will finish growing and change the lives of those he meets.

I'm a single mother locked up in a tower
writing nonsense for those who dare to listen.
But those I wish to share my secrets with
can never stand the madness in me.

I share a bed with many voices
that come and go to their own fulfillment.
They are intrinsic to my spirit, my kin assigned at birth.
Monogamy is only meant to chain
so a single mother I remain.

I am a mother to the unimagined;
words are the only lovers I've ever truly known.
Men become the object of our discussions.
They seek a woman where to find peace
but my spirit is restless like the roots beneath the city streets.

We'll never submit to the demands of silence
not when there is art is growing inside me.

The Life

If you think a writer's life is quiet
think again.

It's assertively troubled
hanging by a thousand threads.

It's a majestic rage
meditating as darts aim at your head.

It's a tortured haven
a baby's cry longing for its mother's breast,
turning safe when paper meets pen.

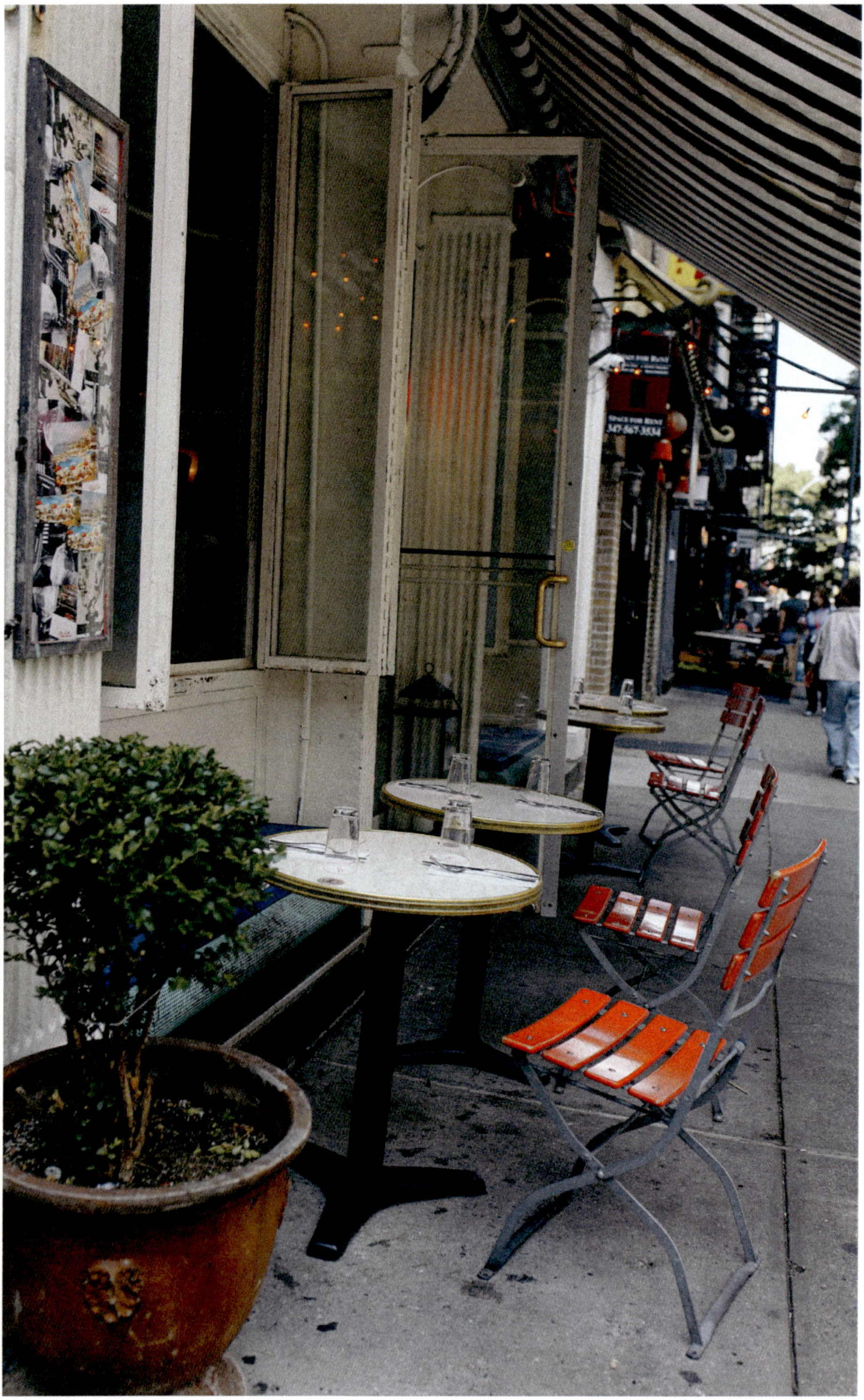

Giving is Hard

I'm a beggar in a corner store, handing out smiles for free.
The more I give, the more pain I receive.

What is the function of my affection
when the child I nurture says the world doesn't deserve me?

Can I keep it stored in a cardboard box
prevent others from drying me out?

I'm afraid if I do, it'll spoil by the time it finds its use.
I'd be a king showered in wealth I cannot share.

So I'll beg and pray that someday
I'll invoke joy instead of pain,
in every corner store I sing.

Guilt-y

I feel small again. I feel lost.
A victim of my own careless thoughts.
I crumble my present
condemning future possibilities
for happiness.

The Wind's Cry

In an instance of doubt the air stops filling my lungs.
I can't breathe, I can't see, I can't think.
Everything distorts inside me.

The peaceful outing turns into a raging sandstorm.
Particles of dust adhere to my pores.

My senses block and magnify my thoughts.
I swirl in a continuous fall.

I cry but the wind cries louder.
She imitates my movements with a stronger force—
one I cannot beat.
I watch it consume me.
I'm not ready like I thought.
I'm weak, I realize
as I repeat to myself, "I'm strong."

I'm not.
I'm tired.
I wish to not hurt.
I wish to be happy and fall in love.
At what cost?
Everything bad happens to me.

Do I bring it on myself with words?

The liberating ones that free me from my chains
invoke new ones as I let the others go.

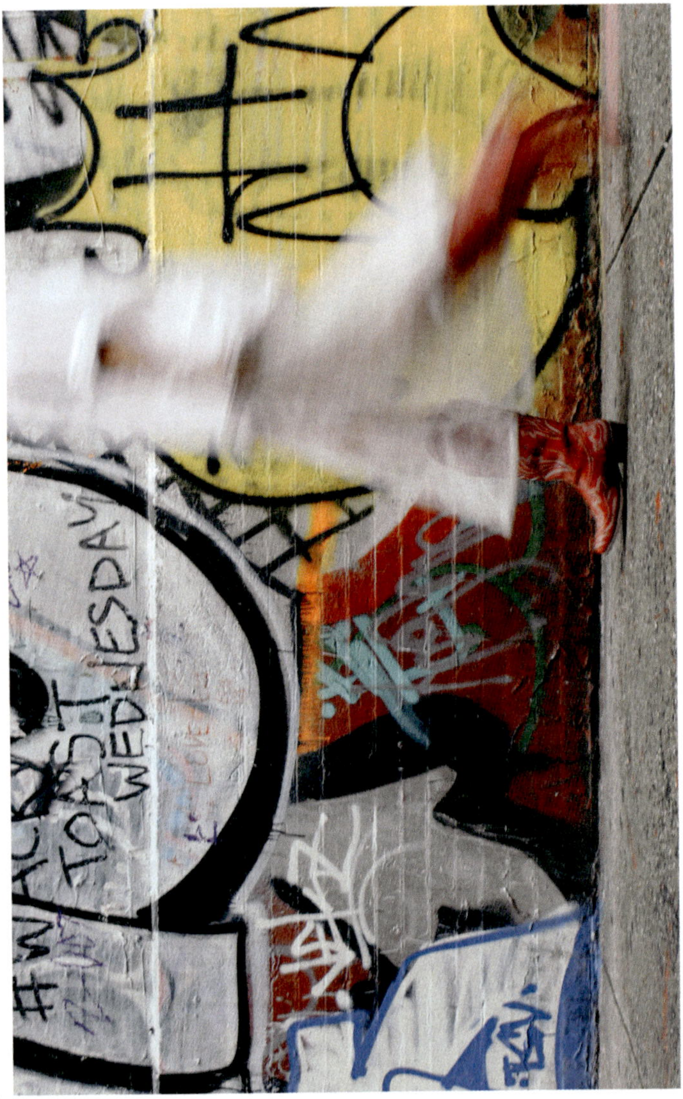
WEDNESDAY

Lingering Sanity

Can I live within the realms of serenity?
If so... when?

Should I hold his hand
or has he grown tired of mine?
The more I breathe
the more I cry.
In clarity I remember the time
I lost my mind.

Will he notice my inadequacies
or will he admire them like he does the urban tapestries?
Get lost in the colors of plastered pain.
The more I breathe
the more I see.
In clarity, I lose perception
of my own sanity.

If in his serene company I await the moment he decides to leave
am I ever at peace?
Will I ever recover my sanity?

Who's the selfish one?

I'm not as tough as I say and need more reassurance than it seems.

If you say "I miss you" today but don't say it again on Sunday
the day after tomorrow I'll assume you learned to live without me.

If you call me today but don't talk to me on Friday
I'll talk less on Saturday,
convinced I overwhelm you with my ranting.

If you say "I love you" today but don't repeat it
every hour of every day
in every thought your mind creates,
I'll believe your heart changed.

Maybe I need more than what I'd like
maybe you give less than what you have.

Perhaps I'm wrong to envy smiles that aren't in my name
perhaps you promised "more"
assuming I'd conform to "enough."

If I sin in greed, I promise to share it all.
I promise your selfish soul will have so much
it won't feel selfish at all.

But in the case my fears have roots
or my petitions become too much,
if the road seems foggy and my light turns dark
say the words and let me go.

In my ears your words still carry truth
and in the distance between us
I refuse to sit here and watch it grow.

Pretty

I've only been loved at night
in the morning comes clarity

I've never been *pretty* under the light.

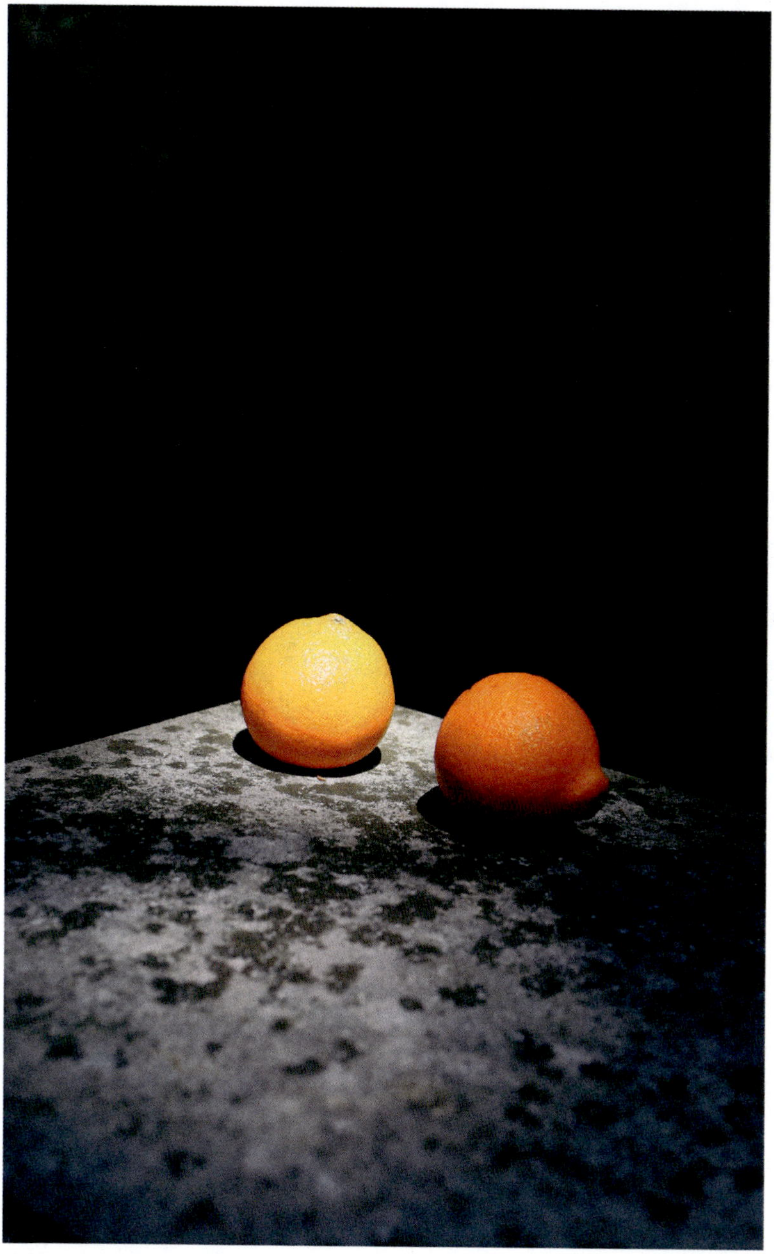

Orange Garnish

Scarcely present when the crowd lays back.
I pierce the halls with poison every time I laugh.

Uninhibited cruelty behind orange peel-garnish
and orange-sliced blue moon beer.

How many records do I have to play
until one turns my sadness away?

If the urban palette wasn't tinted gray
maybe my manners would remember their grace.

But my beauty only comes from the dress I wear
and madness is all I have left to fill it.

Fresh Out of Hugs

Why am I so determined
to find emptiness in loving arms?
My sadness becomes contagious
or maybe love isn't enough.

Can my conviction shift directions
wherever that may take?
My delusions paint with judgment
every glimpse of joy received.

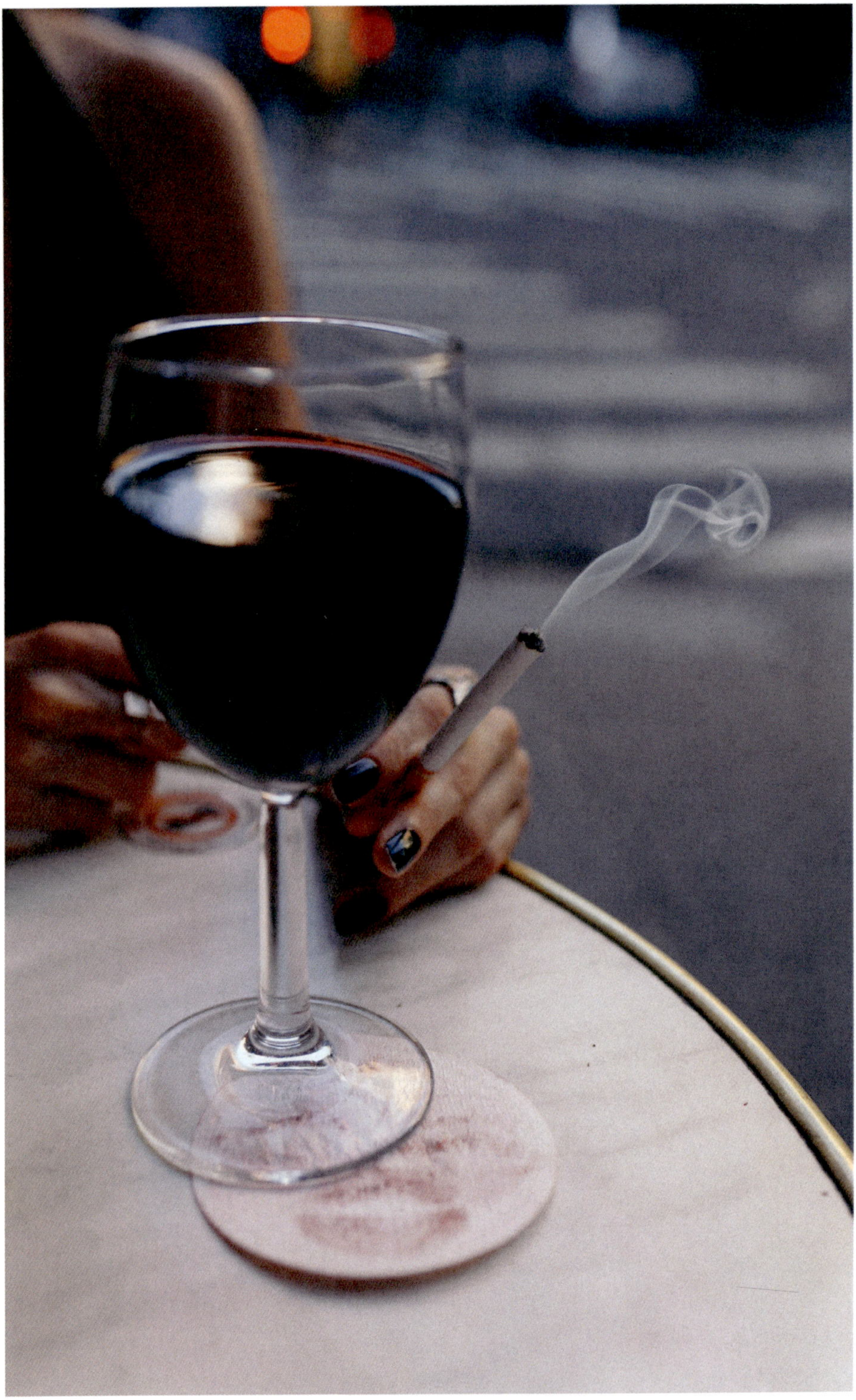

Angelic Gazes

I wish I could see myself
through the eyes of men.

Catch the times
they roll their eyes behind my back
and count the times
their mind pronounces my name.

Frame the liberating words of self-expression
that trigger their queue
to disappear.

"Adiós"

Seal of Confession

I often talk to the mirror
there's no one left to listen
or understand the bitterness
that overrules my optimism.

She replies I'm not good enough—

not good enough a daughter

not good enough a friend

not good enough a lover

not good enough a woman.

It happens often and it makes sense too
who, other than a priest,
enjoys comforting the same *lost* soul?

How can he love
a part of me
I wish would die?

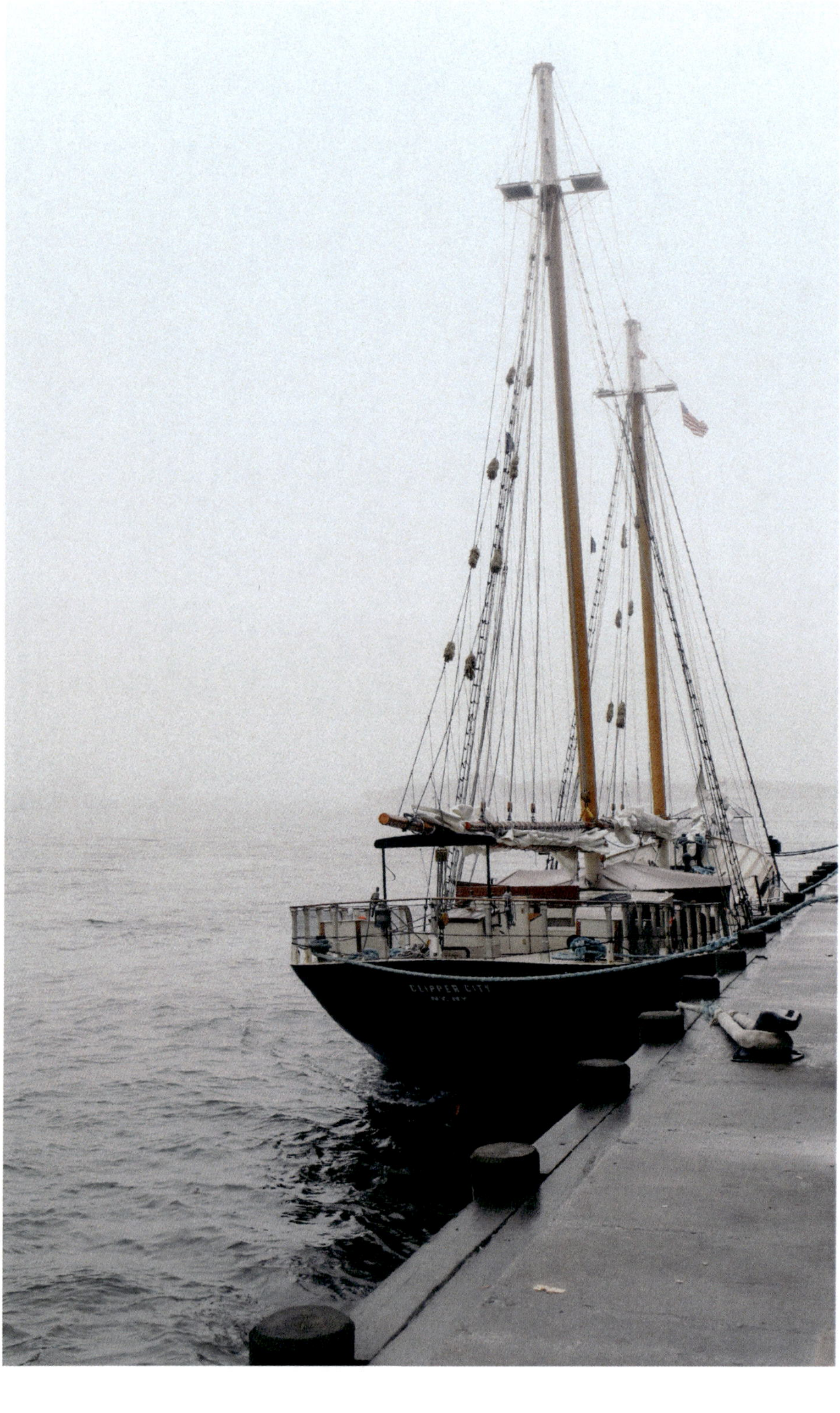
CLIPPER CITY

A Sea of Peace

Am I in the wrong
for demanding instead of letting things flow?
Let the waves overpour their rage
I stand a bullseye in the sand.

Could I be a vessel,
off to find prosperity in different seas?
I anchor myself to fear
wonder why the water kisses me just to leave.

Would you carry me
or watch me sleep and let go?
Let me sink in the depth of an oceanic curse
or dance with me in the rain my eyes provoke.

Is there enough salt
to keep us from rotting while my body floats?
I forgot to swim; I've drowned before.
I stand adrift in soul.

How can I surrender when I'm scared to hurt?
Why am I scared of water when it's the air that drowns my lungs?
When will my fears grow wings?
Which ocean will let me swim in peace?
Who can save me from myself if not me?

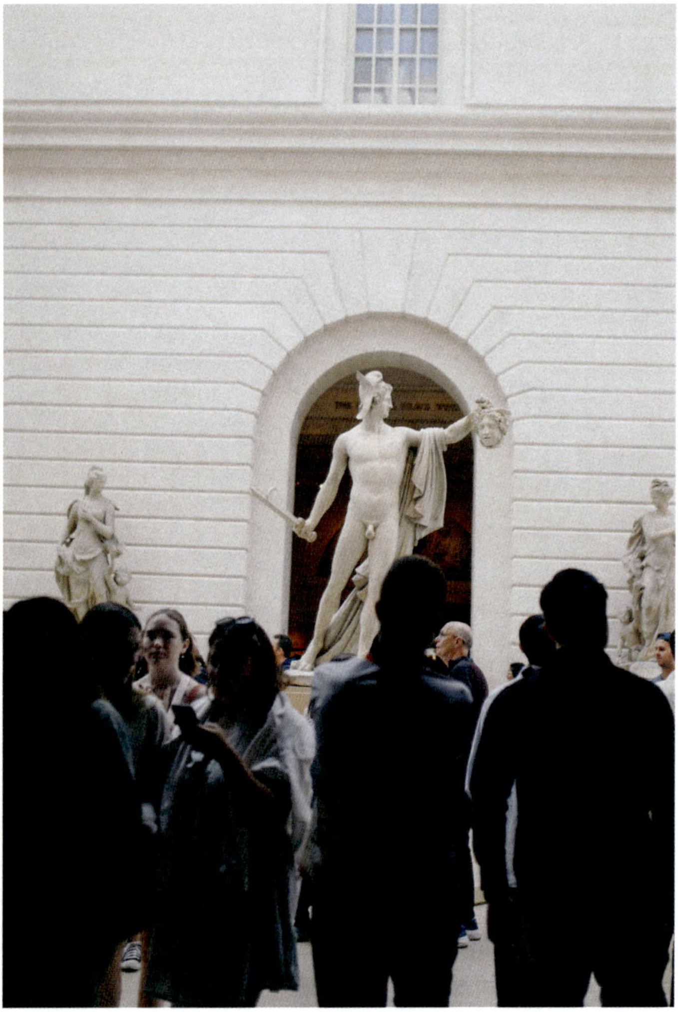

Accurately Inadequate Gossip

What do the elder spirits think of my restless behavior?
I hear their heads shake.

—"You asked for this"
—"She's mad again"
—"She lost her head"
—"She, AGAIN, gave her heart away"
—"That's why the last one left"
—"She never listens"
—"She's got no brain"

Lucky Strike

Did you get pulled on some subway station
or did someone else steal my affection?

Were the words you gave away so freely
never mine to claim?

I tell my head you lost me in the buildings
or some alley the snow washed away.

My lone star state stays the same
while every whiskey's garnished with your name.

Distance tries to make my heart grow fonder
a pistol at my throat to make my screams grow louder.

Lucky you... your roaring thunder
won't let my feelings cloud your laughter.

To Be a Trophy

Men have trophies
rusting on dusty shelves.
His garments pray
to be picked and steamed.
Fresh-cut flowers
die at his careless mercy.

Men don't wear makeup.
But I cover his face with color
the blush that brightens his cheeks
the lipstick that softens his words.

I am the chain that ornaments his neck
the earrings that filter his thoughts
caressing his words, singing his songs.
The bag that carries his insecurities
the stilettos that gracefully absorb his pressures.
I am the hair clip that clears his day of inconveniences
and cling to misjudgment every step we go.

Men don't have accessories.
But to him, I am one.

I am a mere reflection of my embellishments.
So call me brave when I replace my heart with intellect
and sing *I deserve better* to the top of my lungs.
I'm worth a lot.

Should've Listened to Venus

A man once said,
"I am in love with you,"
and there's nothing
Mars,
Jupiter,
or Hell
can do about it.

I followed him
through the rocky roads.
It scratched all my softness,
hanging by the thread
of a promise.

She was born from betrayal and blame; carrying the burden of men's cruelty as a self-inflicting punishment. Love, like water, ran through her fingers and escaped her palms; holding no one responsible other than her flaws. A part of me agreed with her. Since then, I lost complete trust in myself and questioned my deserving of happpiness. I lost sense of what is right and wrong, what are the shoulds and shouldn'ts, which thoughts are real and which are intrusive. And in a blink of an eye, in a misplaced comma, in a dry text message, or a shorter phone call, my confidence flaked. I was again on the ground unable to understand my inability to shape water. She is the ghost I never realized still haunted me, unable to rest in peace within eternity. At the very least, I learned the truth of my flaws; baggage I refuse to carry in my own home.

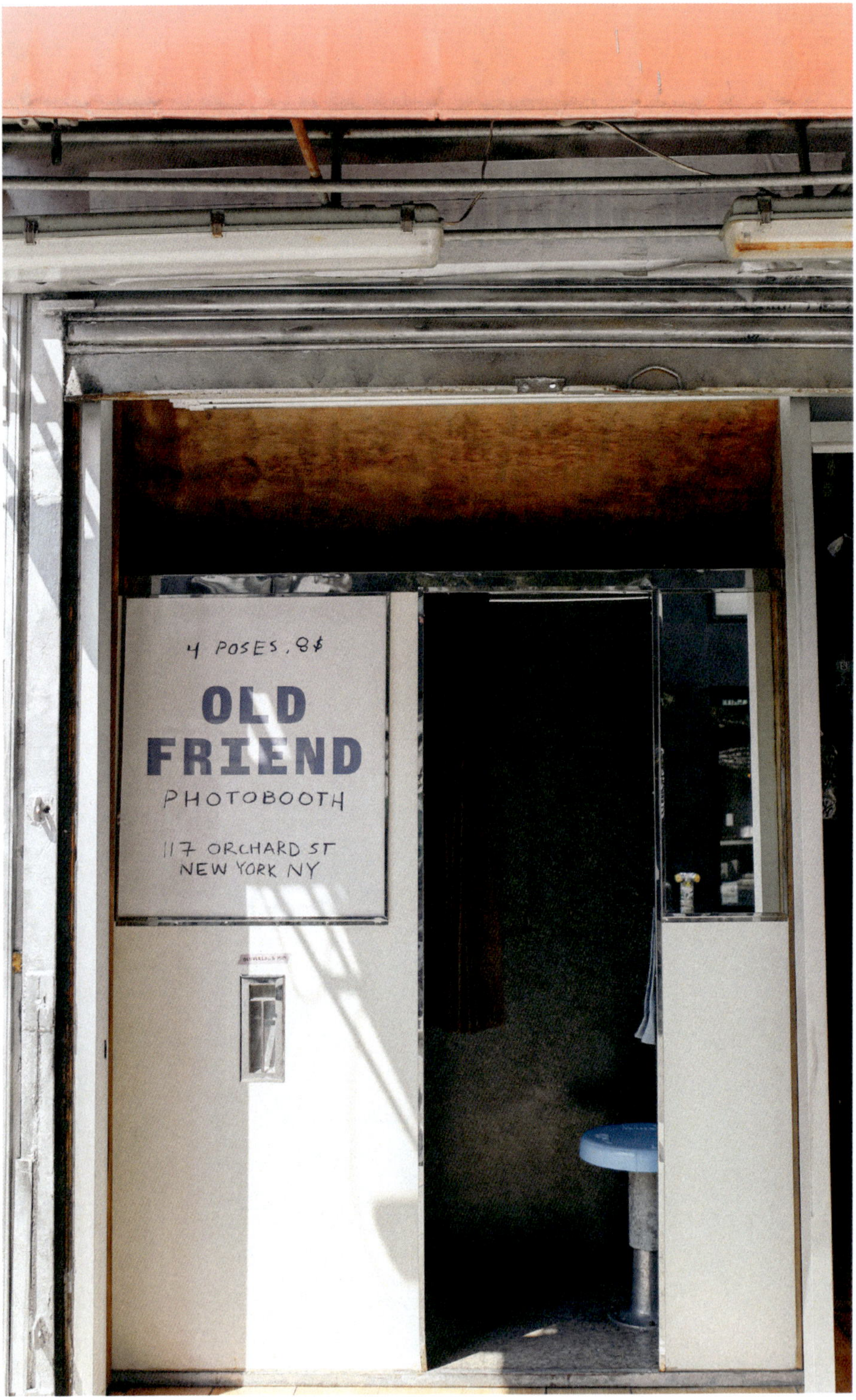
4 POSES, 8$
OLD
FRIEND
PHOTOBOOTH
117 ORCHARD ST
NEW YORK NY

Never Enough

A tear streams down the left side of my eye.
I've said I'm too much before
I've never shown you why.

I feel so much, too much—
I feel for both of us.

I share my ability
my passion to feel.
But all you see is liability
an unstable wheel.

My eyes wander into different worlds.
They see meaning behind scars
and art in thoughts that hurt.

In efforts to dim my fire
I only throttle back our flame.

Now you see my spark as a burden
and these eyes will burn, for yours
can't understand my poetry.

A second tear streams down the left side of my eye.
I've said enough already
and my mind has grown shy.

If this makes me a lot
I'm sorry you're not.

I'm a lot
I'm too much, so much
but still never enough
for what could've been both of us.

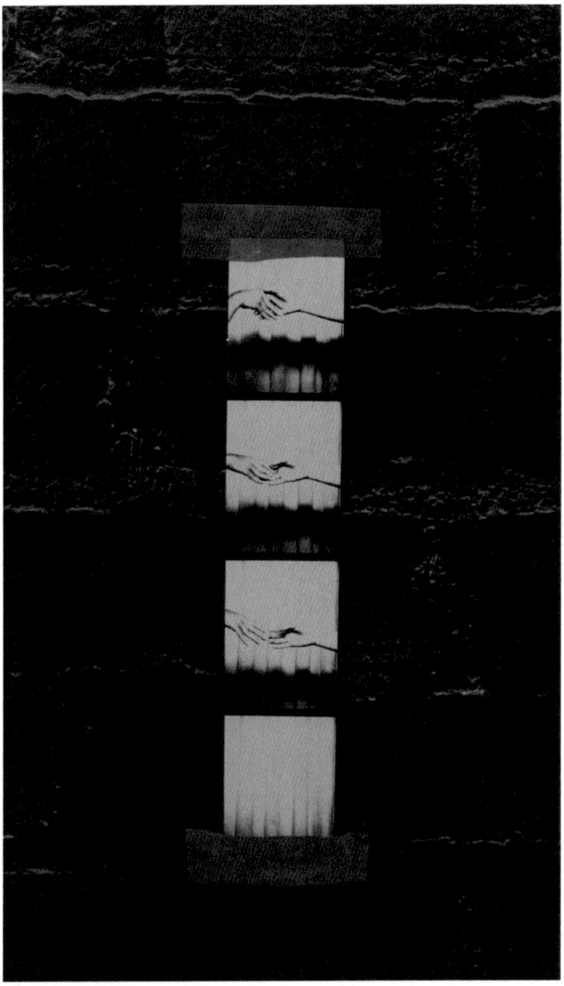

The Burden

Remember the day you said my presence
could never become a burden?
If my absence brings relief
then you stand corrected.

And I'll stand unaffected.
Your words, once sweet, can salt my tears
but will never intensify the weight of my rotting fears.

Lost Tribeca

The windowless room shrinks with each mistimed glare
while our tongues hold hostage the other's courage.

My legs— a concrete sculpture
when the lender came
to collect a debt for the time borrowed.

One last fist to retrieve
the love laid on the sheets;
what's left will expire
on the next bodies they'll cover.

Stubborn conviction to bet on love
when the players have a broken heart.

Your hand will never lay on my breast as we read
and I'll miss holding New York while it falls asleep.

Stripped from promises,
I dress with indifference the urge to stay
before you cowardly looked away.

Let the doorknob mourn
the indelible memories Tribeca gained
when our trifecta bet lost.

Say "Cheese"

The walls relinquish mockery.
How could they foresee a louder silence
than the one they were built to contain?

The monsters grew fond of your suffocating ivy,
intertwined bullets aimed at the stars—
shot the sun and moon.

Bricks incite fake condolences
old fears silence honest words
barricaded by each other's demons.

Windowless inferno trapped in a meadow
making up lies to justify
the premature end of an anticipated fall.

Quiet, still, smile, *flash*—

we're past.

BAYARD ST

ONE WAY

212-227-4888

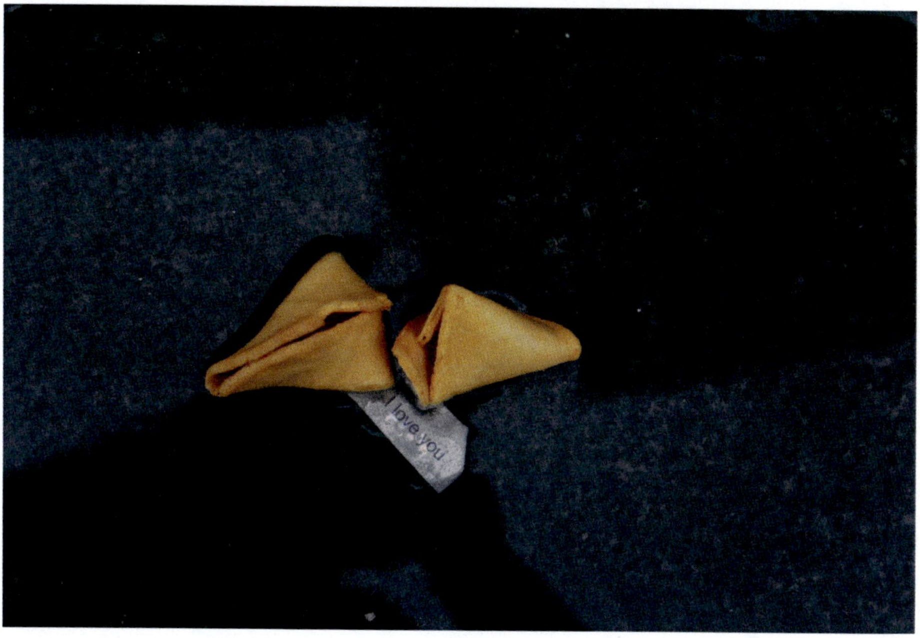
I love you

Art Imitates Life

I'd scream
but there's no one left to listen.
My rage
blends with the city's choir.
At least
my sadness
blends with something
others can admire.

Empty Eyes

I suddenly look different
when their love for me goes away.
It scares me because I remained the same—
It means they never loved me for *me*
in the first place.

Over the Moon

The monsters laugh in pity while shadows creep away.
They fear the gentlest draft
will kidnap my last ray of light.

But compared to passengers
who've grown deaf in heart,
my spirit stays youthful
stationed in Brooklyn Bridge City Hall.

Time never ticks loud enough to scare me off.
I'm done
I'm young
I'm yours.
Until the next train comes along
      the next city
      the next dodge.
      The trumpets of a sun to praise my stains
            to raise my blinds
                to draw my shadow back.

TRACK 24

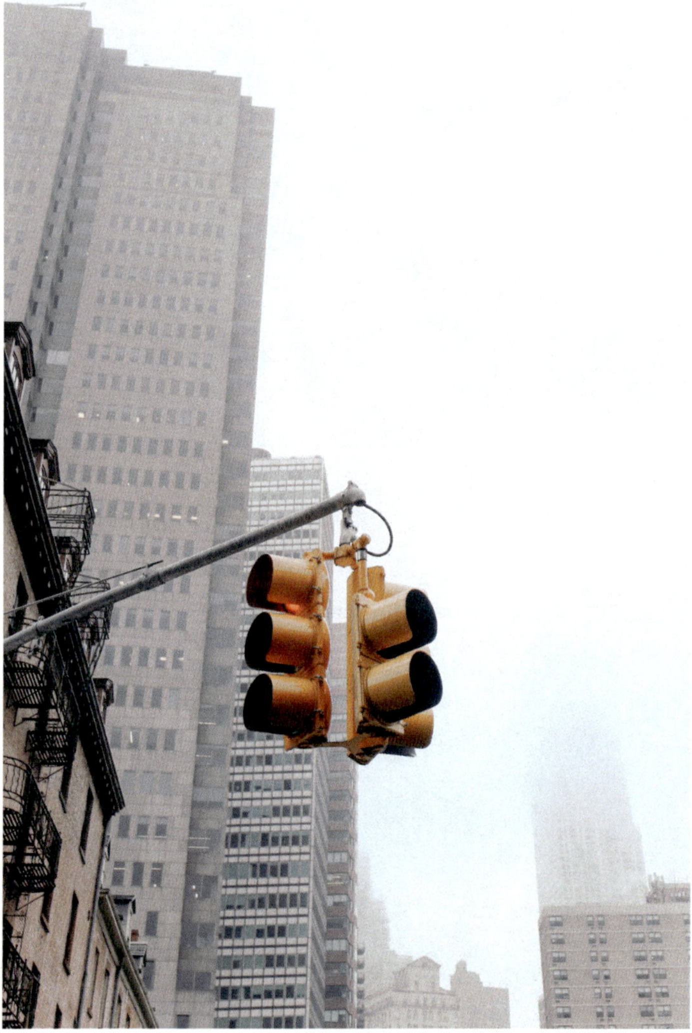

In the Left I am Left

A corpse roams around the city
—"Watch out, the queen is dead!"

Rotting started at the center
made its way to my stomach; hunger's left.

—"Beware, she's right!"
I'm thin again, collecting crumbs of affection to survive.

My heels point North, but don't bleed anymore
my bones are bent, and my soul turned South.

The Realms that Divide Us

Once, you and I were kings and queens of different realms.
In time our love bloomed; in our absence it grew.

Our empty nests nurtured ambition inside fragile shells
where the free birds of optimism sang.

But the lands we united divided our suns and space.
I slept with crowds for beers and bottles—
voices rumbled, none as deep as yours.

Much left to say, if only there was a mouth
brave enough to risk the safety silence covers us with.

Only the tears the other is too far to see
will feed the birdies in our sycamore tree.

So, at dinner parties
when you find the empty seat
let the lies sit.

Share the story of how you wove yourself into my sheets.
All this to feel,
how much love a loveless artist could seed.

But the blind will see the truth
a king only loses when he lets the queen go.

Can Time be Kind?

And the streets in Texas cry
when the clock strikes past midnight.
They wait to hear your voice
never thought I'd be gone first.

And now that New York City's quiet
when the clock's hands punch your gut,
send a prayer so your voice
echoes my heart.

STARS ALIGN

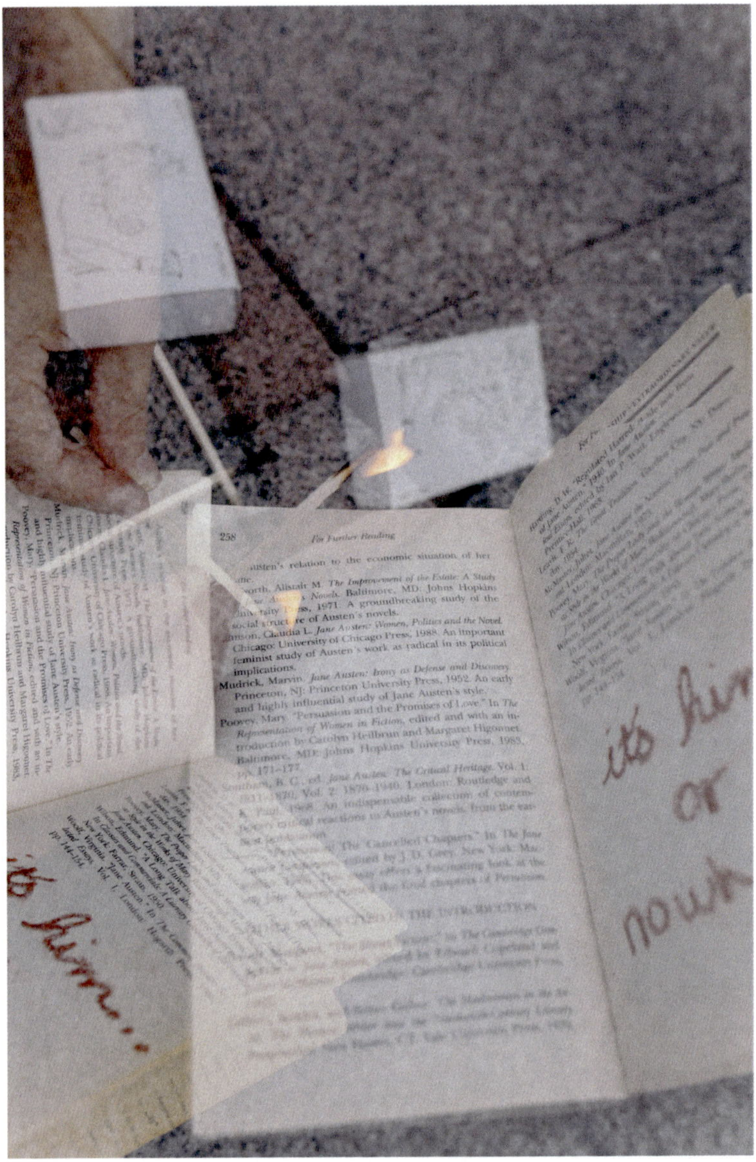

Flames of Cool

Livelihood is the means to a healthy mind.
As my hair grows
my insides burst in freezing flames.

109°F Texas heat isn't enough
to soften a heart made of bones.

The polite gestures exchanged
only ignite fire that breathes with unfulfillment.

Sustenance belongs to a heart that drops
a body that craves a love that is lost.

But only a corpse can leave with grace
remain warm as the snow drapes the city
and shiver while the sun melts my sins.

I am not cold.
I am not warm.

I suffocate as parts of me slowly die.

Makes Sense

I find it easier
to love others
than to love myself
with that same depth.

The most
important person
I should care for
is the one
I most neglect.

I never question
when a man
decides to leave
I agree
they'd be better off
without me.

The Sound of Leaves

I wonder where I can find
the person who decided my emptiness
should be measured with blessings in disguise.

I got lost in the city's veins looking for his heart
drowning more and more in its blood.

I can't distinguish the vicious cycle I walk in.
I'm blind again.

I notice the urban calm outside my door—
the recurring traffic noises, and occasional dog bark.

Friends laugh at jokes I don't find funny
unable to relieve symptoms of an incurable disease.

My beauty decays in the peak of its youth
only appeal to eyes that steal what little is left in me.

Is there a prophecy defaming my core's wickedness?
To stay is treachery when it's time to leave.

My numbness grows; only my stomach sickens.
Wine is the only nutrient well received by my throat.

Jimmy asked to dance, but all I think is when
I'll again hear the sound of leaves hanging on trees—

without it, I become nothing.
There is nothing in me.

It was in this epiphany that I understood goodbyes are necessary, that the man who long ago hurt me did not lie when he said love isn't always enough. Love is an action, a practice, a determination. It requires dedication and consistency, qualities only found within the conviction to become better at it. I'm not ready for that—not when she is still alive and present inside me.

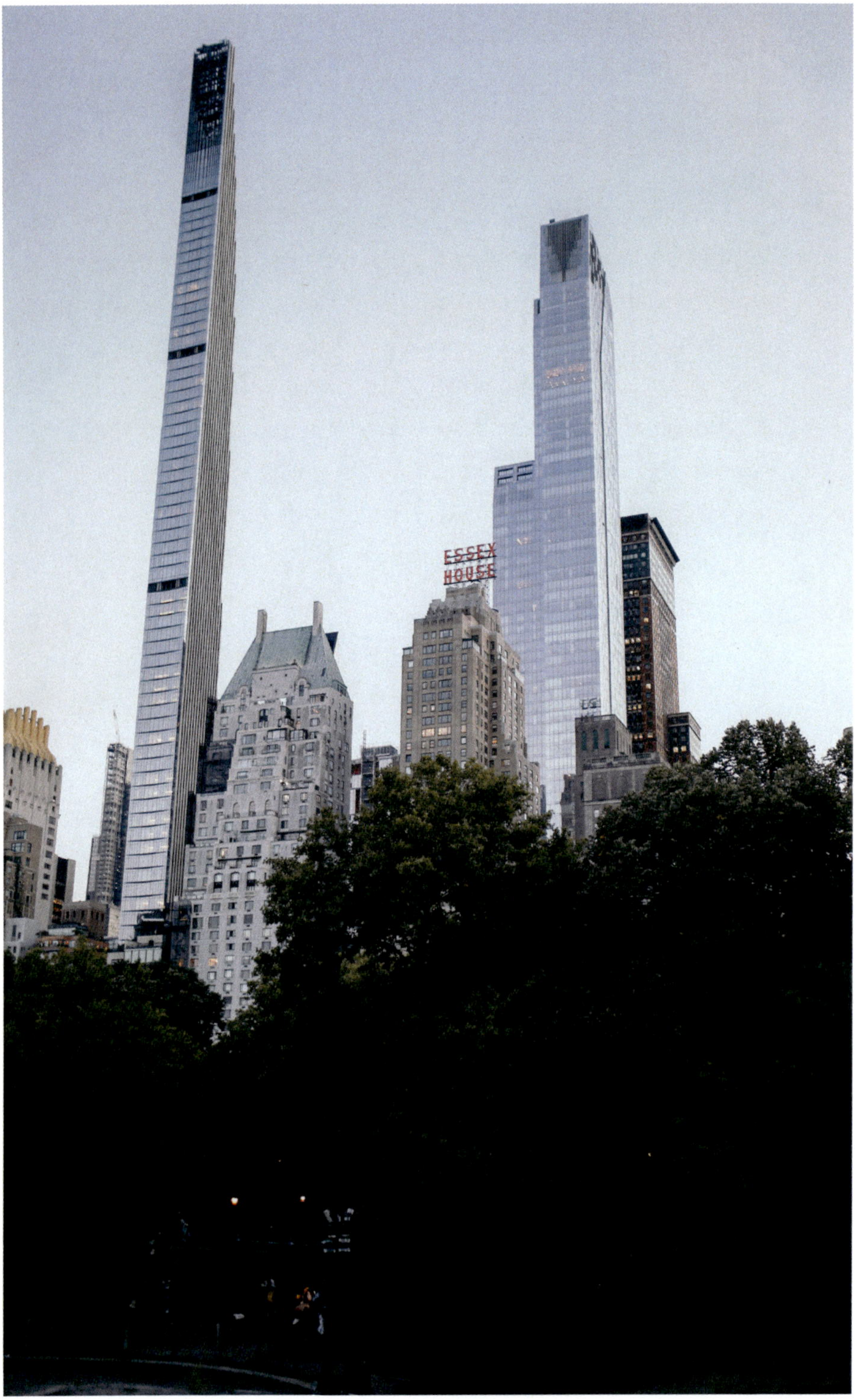
ESSEX
HOUSE

Exhaling Freedom

I always refused to cut my long hair
let it grow and grow
always so eager to cut pieces of me
for the angels that walked my door.

I like Lana...
"Well, I like Janis more."
So, I danced to Janis until she became my favorite song.

I like summer...
"Well, I like winter more."
So, I wore underlayers to mask the frostbite in my bones.

I like to smoke...
"Well, that's no way to mother our children."
So, I surrendered my will for a future we might share.

I like New York...
"Well, what's a silly girl like you gonna do there?"
So, I caged my dreams for words that looked like promise rings.

Covered in hair my spirit shivers,
like broken blinds lingering to the first rays of summer.

Fever Dreams

I've never found solace
in solitude.
What a wonderful skill that must be—
to sit at peace
and become one with eternity.

The Travels of Voices

My thoughts extend wider
than the arms of God
and always bring back a map
as a souvenir.

From Texas to New York
across the deserted roads
embellished with lonely billboards
tumbleweeds, and horse-drawn cabs,
they land.

From December to January
in the yearning that holds us together
the song I skip in the record I play
as close as a year's-ago instance,
they land.

From Thanksgiving to New Year's Day
beneath the prayers and the snow
in the shoulder I relied on
before spring turned it cold,
they land.

From the knife in my pen
to the bullets in your silence
mediating a cold war
crusaded with cowardice.

In the door I opened
while for you it closed, they land.

Naive Little Girl

I know nothing, and nothing knows me.
But if I knew one thing:
I'm never the one that got away.

Quite the opposite, I always stay.
Our roots ground my love for him
despite the sickening weeds they sprout.

Words from the heart are louder for poets.
So when the barrel meets the bottom
and the singer leaves the stage,

a part of me stays inside the room
in case he might someday return.

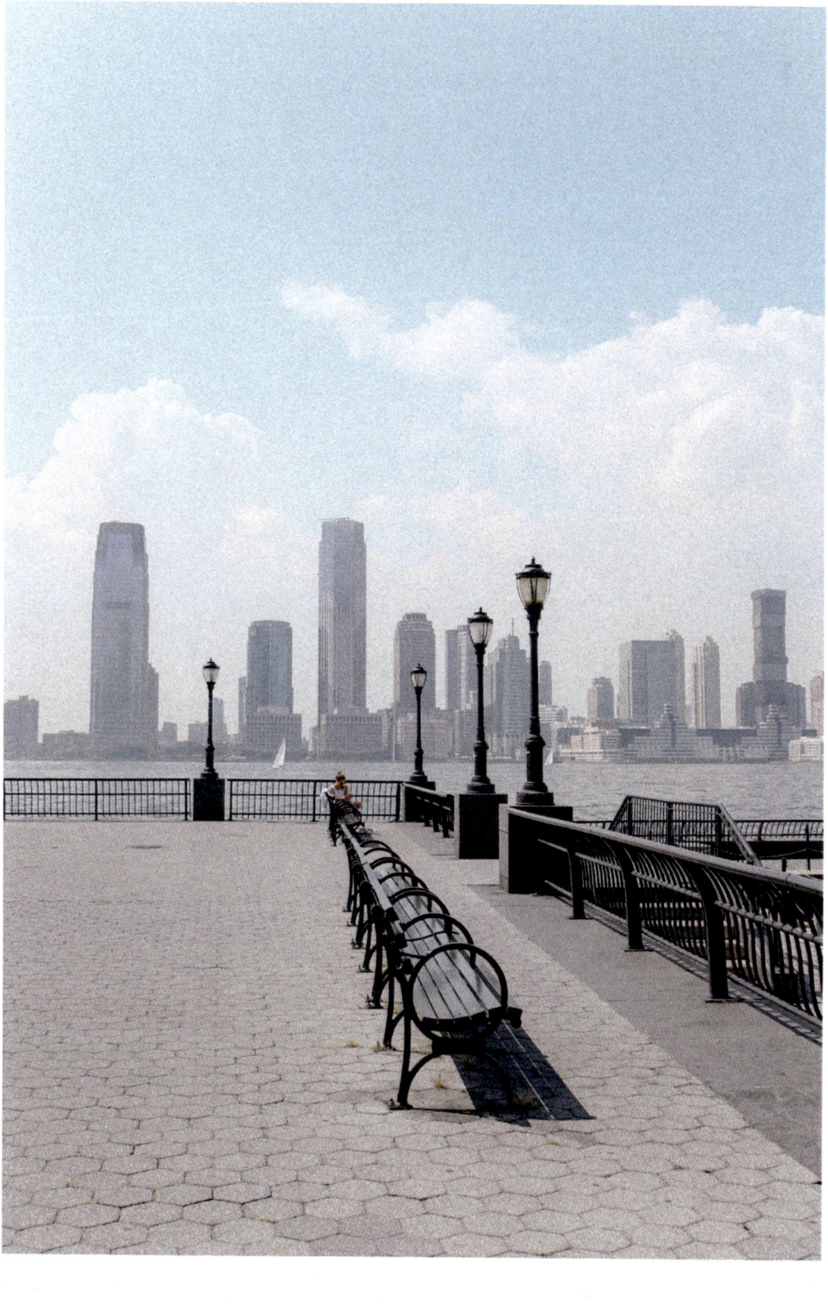

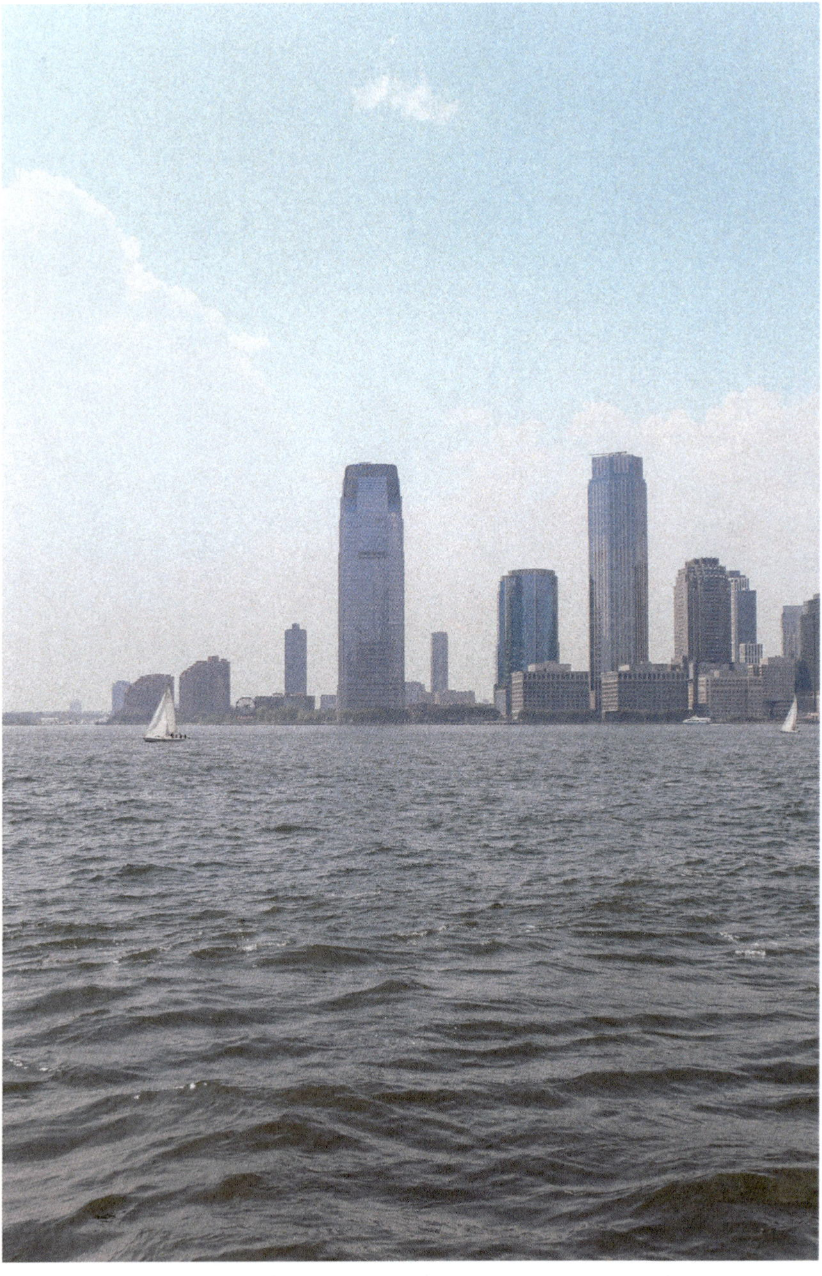

Peace Offerings

I'm a stone collector—
pick one up everywhere I go.

Something to offer the sea
when I meet her shores.

She'll be the death of me;
I refuse to let my past go.

Cheats & Barren Fields

It's in crowded places I long for your company most,
where lustful eyes entertain self-absorbed tongues
and crude awakenings put to bed endearing words.

It's in crowded places where everyone looks for truth.
Forced indifference poisons the air with make-believe allures
to feel the high of the body, at the cost of a soul.

It's in crowded places where I settle collecting parts of you
like a stray dog digging for gold in the scum,
devouring liquor to numb the disappointing search.

It's in crowded places where men put their lies to practice.
I bat my eyes to play along with their charade
repulsed by the affection I conform to.

Here I wonder how big a fight our love deserved.
I'm afraid I let go of something whole
wonder if, in crowded places, you draw the same conclusion too.

My Hoping Fades

I'd go sit at the bar and wait around
see if your loneliness drives you there too.
Instead, I'll lock the door
with monsters I'm familiar with,
and hope I can forget you
before the day you return home.

Love Song

I wanted you to be my love song
I only know how to write sad ones.

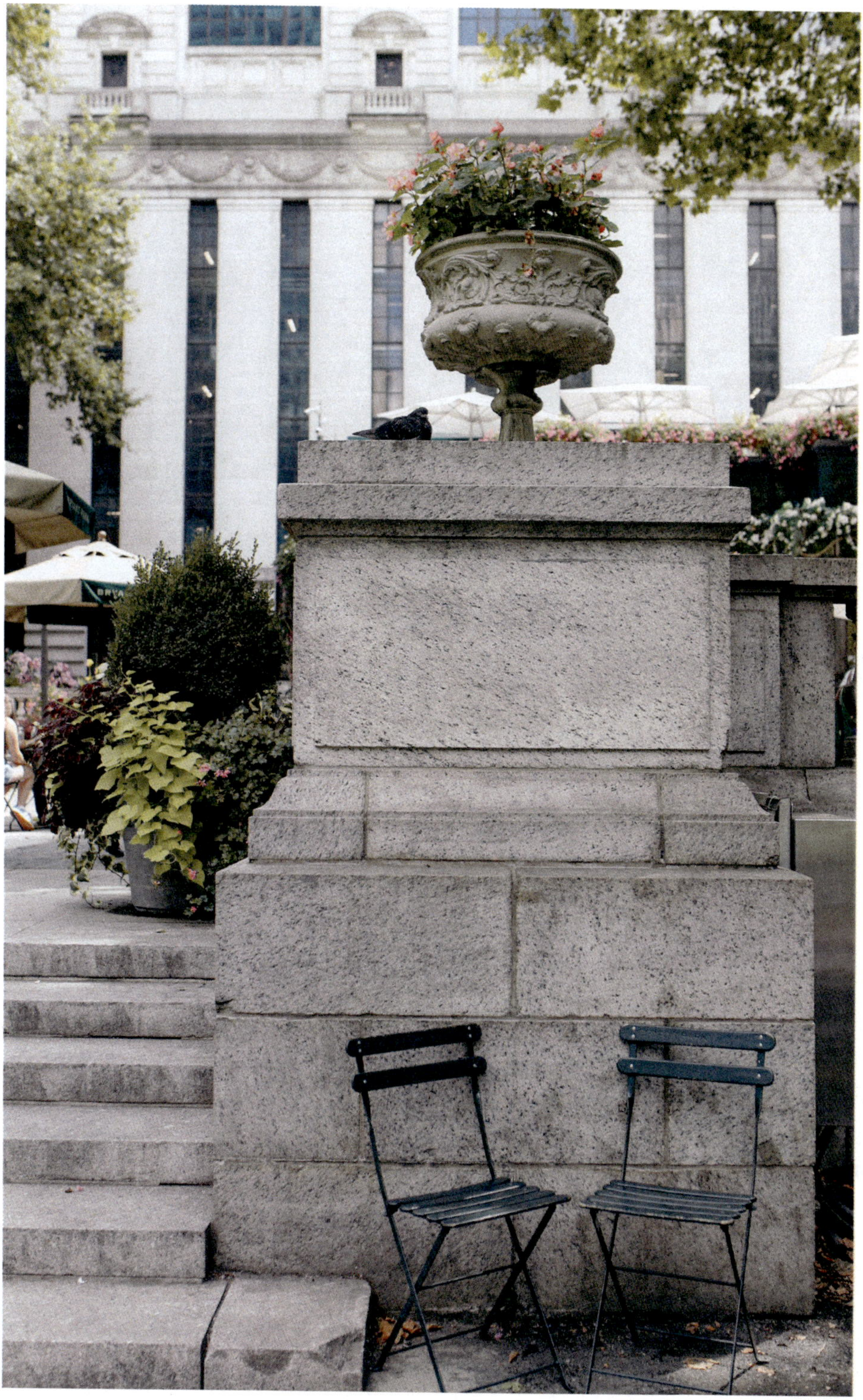

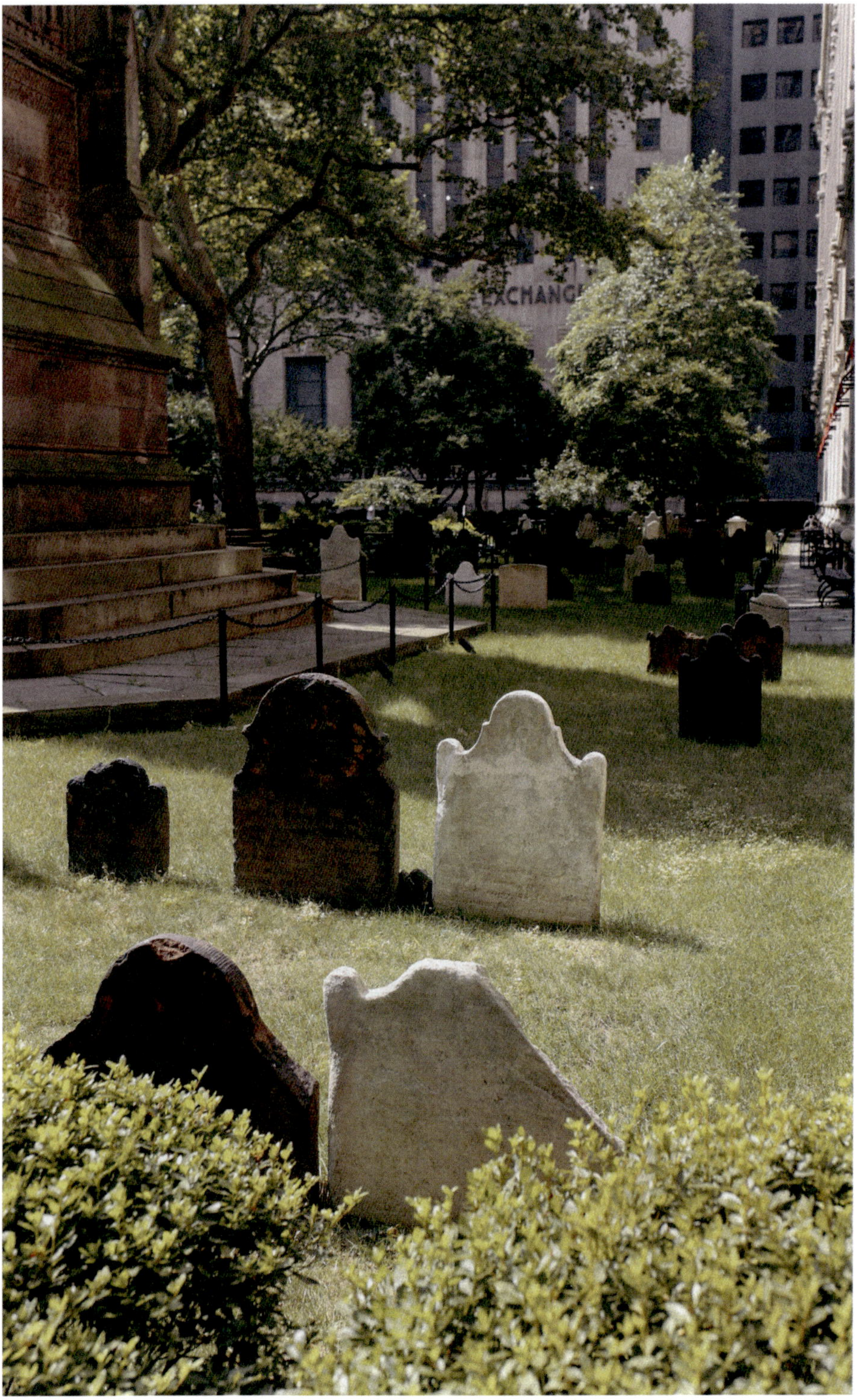
EXCHANG

November Rain

November carries the 4th year of an angel's absence.
It marks the 3rd year of another's crime
and the 2nd year of a blessing I hope bears no disguise.

In November I cry; the flowers died.
I reopen books with petals of different bouquets.
They protect stories I'm devoted to forget.

In my repertoire of memories
melancholy coats the bright pictures bitter
and the unbearable ones trap me in their pain.

In November the sun's visits become shorter.
My prayers become longer; my cries grow louder—
it's the only month I go to church.

In November roots turn to stones
for people who left without death.
I'm a leaf falling from a tree, waiting to bloom again in spring.

Tears of Wisdom

What would Daddy say
to see a wealthy man beg
to see a racehorse profess he's lame.

But if life is made of cycles
can I be allowed to be sad once in a while?
Shed tears for a song I can't play
hurt for the people who decide not to stay.

I'd pack my things
and mourn with spring
pretend I don't care
for those who didn't care about me.

But if I'm to leave those feelings behind
who's to feel what I have inside?
Mourn the lies I naively believed
bury a love that refuses to die.

What would my moral compass say if he saw me stay
if he saw a boxer let one more rib break
if he saw a singer play an empty stage.

Until heavenly tears
carry words instead of rain
I'll pretend he says:

*Cowards in time might reek contempt
but only courage will always breed content.*

Wildflower

Strengthless will of conviction,

render spirits that flower wildflowers
amongst the contempt of well-kept roses.

—"Your petals lack livelihood,"
cheeks that don't blush
stems that don't curve to greet the sun.

—"Relinquish your beauty to the man who waters you."
Ashes don't impress the splendor of wealth
when the queen's off with the head of mad hatters, parading doubt.

Stand in pride;
no sun greeted your birth.
You saw lessons in barren fields and proved the world wrong.

Irrefutable miracle to be nurtured by pain.
Petals shouldn't blush
on a flower that blooms with blood.

Your existence is proof of life bigger than love.

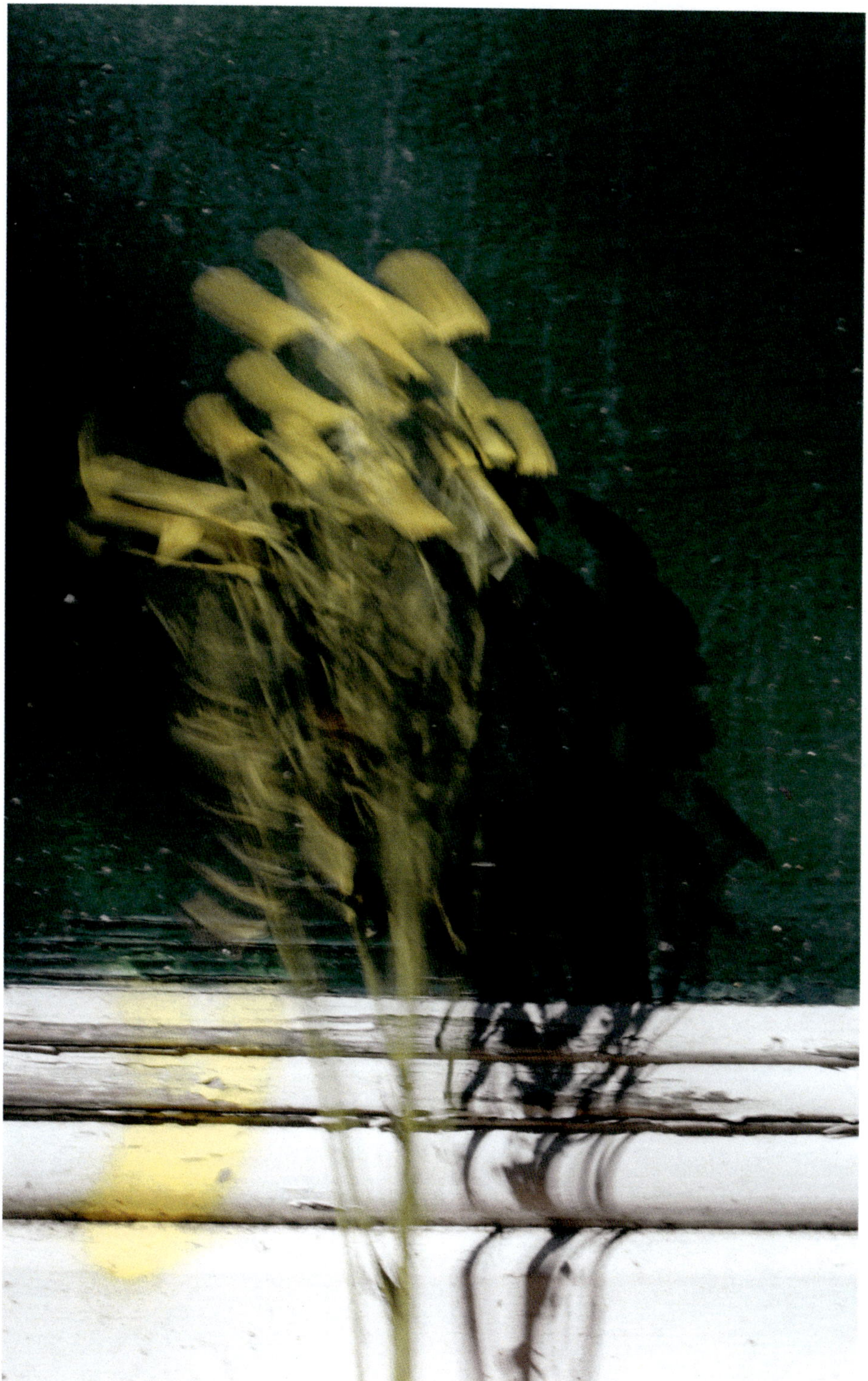

I Vow

Those who care for me ask
why do I still care for you?

Their confused disapproval
fails to grasp the vows I made to Love.

Not the romantic one I once desperately clung to
or the one that fades,
when a misconstrued perception of beauty changes
but the one that shares without strings attached.

I made a vow to love
with nothing more
and nothing less
then all my essence has.

To overpour and splatter
those I meet,
handing out pieces... for *free*.

Yours was the pleasure
mine was the privilege
ours are the moments

unconditional.

I will always be ignorant of the amount of blame the interference of my past had with the man I went to see. He wasn't innocent either, but that's a chapter I have no interest in revisiting while I heal. We will never know how much blame should be divided among us, nor do I think we care. It takes encountering love to understand our inability to practice it, just like it takes trying to run a marathon to realize you can only run a mile. Picking up an instrument to understand you can only play certain keys, and picking up a person to understand you can only carry so much of them or for so long.

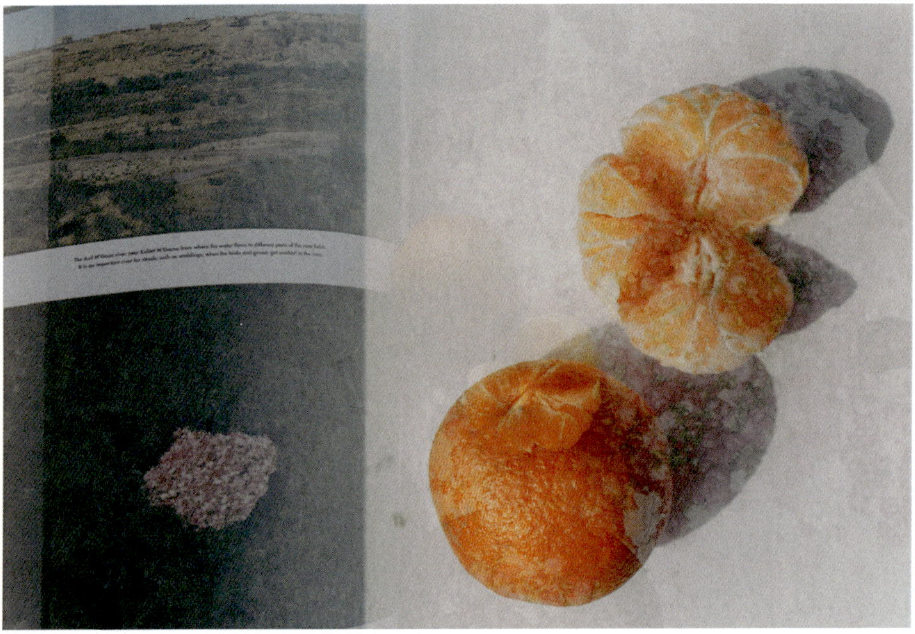

Lifeblood

My love is not a reflection of those I love
but of my capacity to love—
to feel
to give.
I choose to love with all I am, with all I have.

What am I?
I am my words, my mind,
my energy, my time.

I love you in every word I write
in every thought that carries your name
in all the energy I let you take
in all the time I let you spend.

My love is as generous as the Texas heat,
fiercely grieving with its same intensity.

Yet, I never wish to love any less than I already do.
If anything, I wish to love even more.
In everything you take
I pray I make more to give.

My love is a fountain of abundance—
such abundance my hurt will not persist,
nor your taking discourage
my will to give.

To think I'd conform to your absence
was a selfish trick you pulled

                              to ask for more was my selfish response to you.

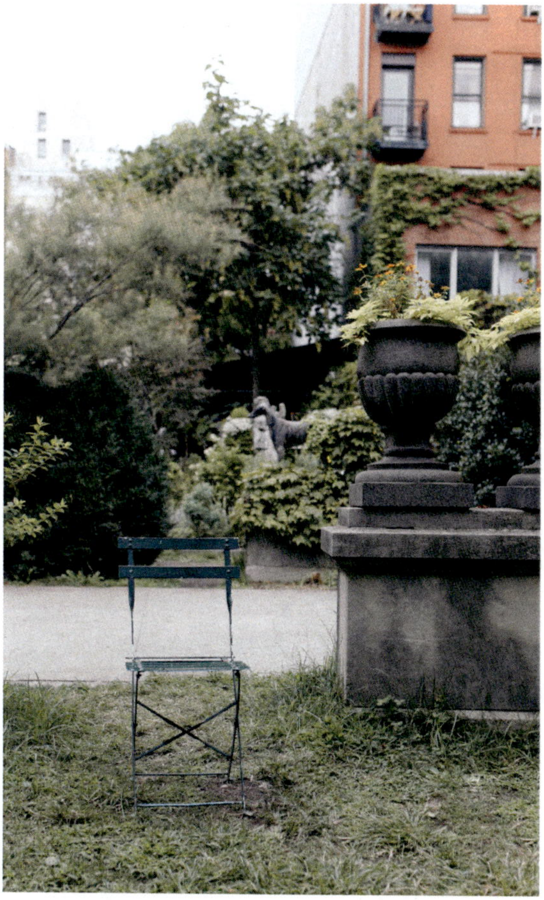

When Regret Knocks

Had I known you'd be gone
I would've taken more of you.
Left my integrity behind
and savored the last minute
I was still allowed
to call you mine.

Wreckful Wonder

I miss the same way I love—
to the bone, in the blood.
Forceful chains of reminiscence
that oppress my lungs.

I look for you in stop lights
and see you in others' empty stares.
Drawing conversations out of thin air
to cautiously craft your reply.

My heart deliriously races
is it you behind the Silverado?
I let your absence become significant.
How else am I to show my undying love for you?

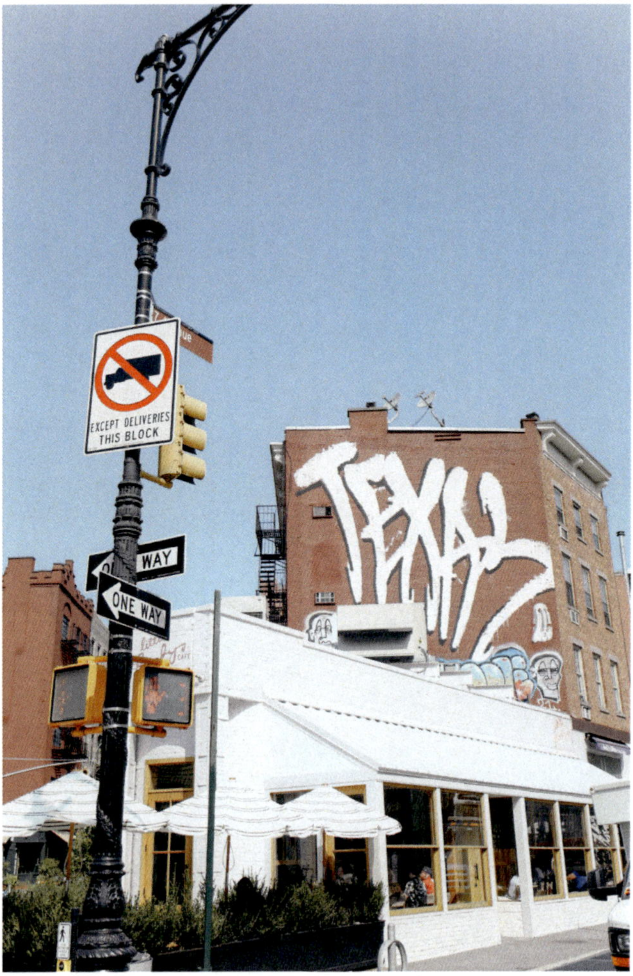
EXCEPT DELIVERIES
THIS BLOCK
WAY
ONE WAY

Urban Cowboys

In wanderlust evenings, the cowboys greet the fields
of concrete charades and orange-squeezed beers.
They wear their hats like crowns
and hospitality like a two-person saddle.

My urban cowboy, come back to the open roads of roses
where visions of dreams ornament the silence.
—*My solitude now has company.*

Is it fair to ask if you miss me in the crowds
in the fighters or the clowns?
Are the fame beggars and parasites of joy
as entertaining as our midnight rodeos were?

Am I the poet selling pieces of my body, so we won't starve?
Like the singer whose voice blooms when the blue light shines.
Or am I the overrun racehorse with no limbs left
but his unsold heart?

I was once special in wanderlust evenings
but there's only so much a desert ghost can offer.
So when the girls up North braid their hair with thornless flowers
remember the gardens I cleaned
to keep your fingers from scratching.

Blues are the result
of my own inadequacy
to fulfill my heart.

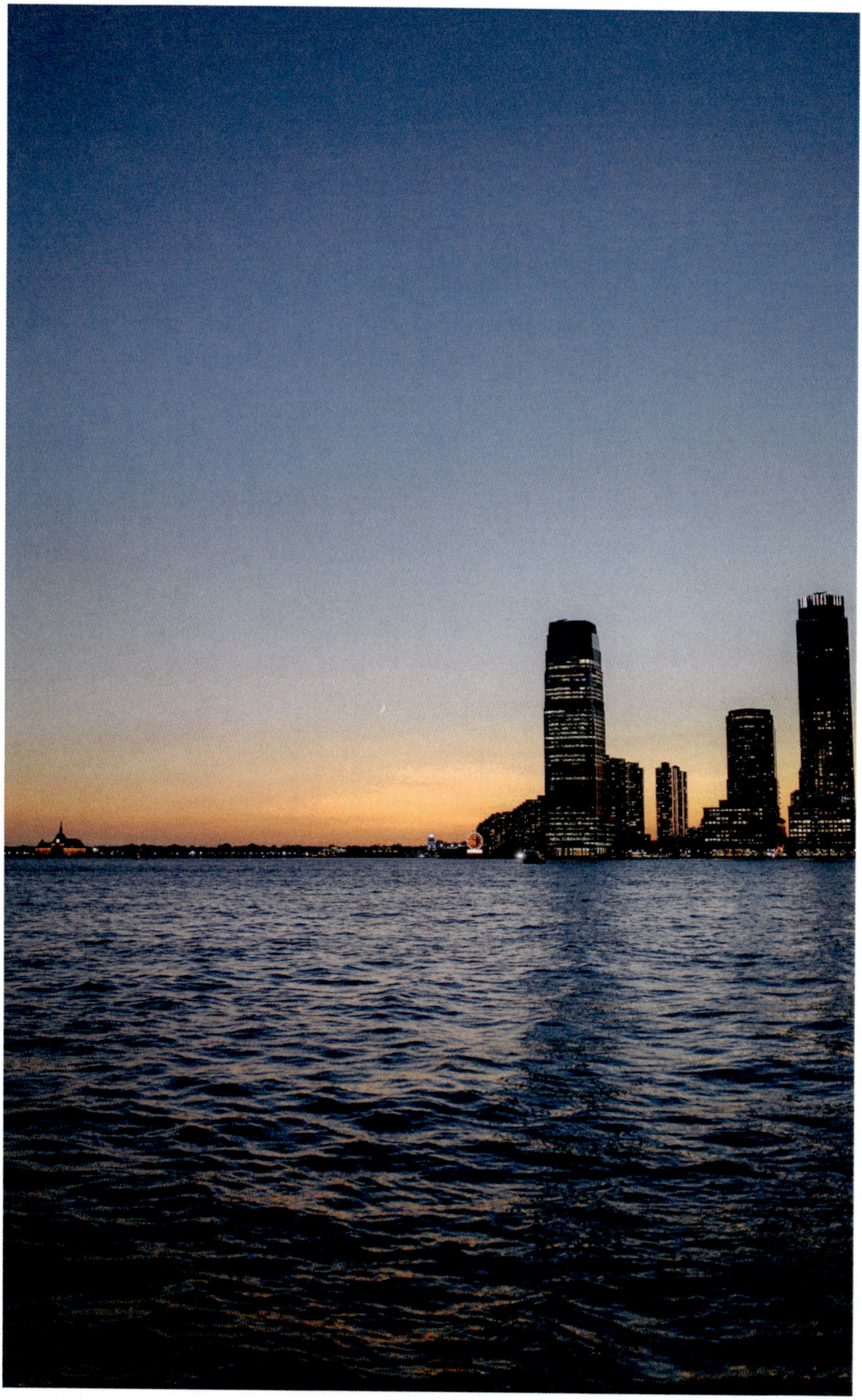

What if...
smoking was rejuvenating, and longing was a sin?
We'd grow old together, dreading the end.

What if...
we reserved each other for letters,
and avoided inconvenient phones?
—"Dear, I like carrot cake too." January 17th, 1974

What if...
soul wounds were replaced with paper cuts?
I'd believe in band-aids, but the absent cracks inside us
wouldn't let the other's light in.

What if...
mirrors reflected the naked heart instead?
You'd be as beautiful, if not more,
and I'd pump ink instead of blood.

What if...
aiming guns eased anxiety?
We'd supply ammunition in secrets, hopes, and dreams
pull the trigger for a shot at peace.

What if...
instead of Texas, it was New York?
I'd never be able to prove that in growing distances
and lack of shared instances,
your soul will always reach my words.

Is It the End?

How many endings has the corner street witnessed—
the one that gave birth to our fresh beginning?

How long until we begin again
on a different holiday or a different city?

A Penny's Worth

Remember those singing for pennies in the park?
"Freedom's just another word for nothing left to lose."
If you're no longer mine, why do I keep flying back to you?

I'm no longer yours either; Reed and I went for a walk.
But I find myself singing to every window in New York City
to see if my words still reach your thoughts.

The lights here at night glow brighter than the desert rise.
I see couples fight in the alleys outside the clubs
while *friends* walk into bars, ordering drinks to buy the other's love.

I simply stand and wonder how we never became either of those.
Less were the times I saw you than the nights I dreamed you
now I sit and read to the park about our misfortune.

My body's free to roam
but my mind only walks to places it can find you.
So I'll sit at the bar, let Reed buy me a drink
and for a penny of a second... pretend it's you and not him.

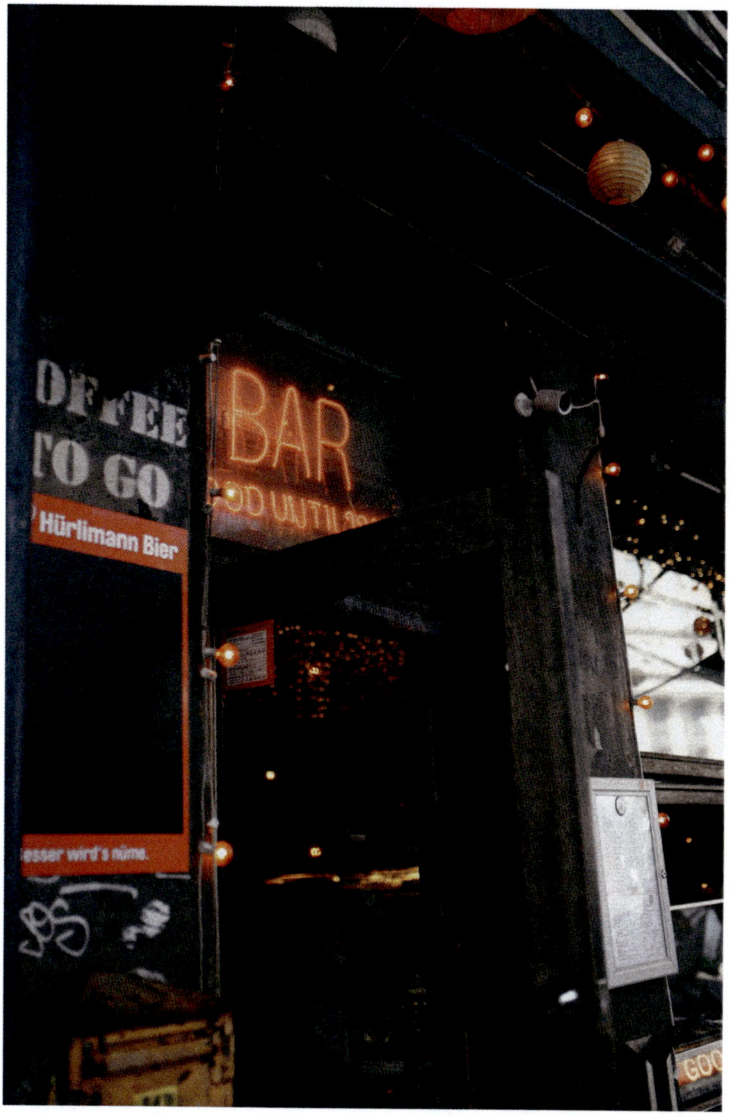
TO GO
Hürlimann Bier
BAR

Nested in Oblivion

Only when I write do I forget
how entrapped I am inside my head.

Only when I write do I become ideas
and live inside the ink and pen.

Thoughts become bigger than me
the masters to my slave.

Only in mindful clarity do I fly without rising
confined to the walls of a city,
like a bird who refuses to leave the nest.

Dear Lord,

I only ask you to take his pain away.
I don't care about mine anymore.
All I care about is for him to be okay.

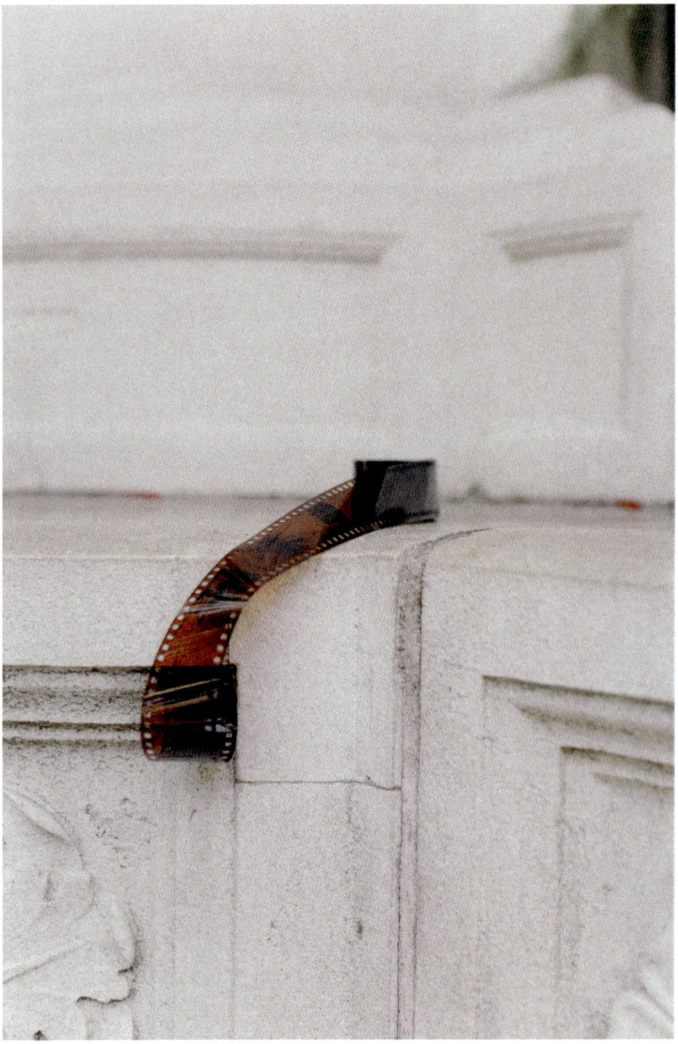

Reminiscence

I've asked my mind so many times
to let your memory go.
She refuses to render her will;
thinks I should treasure
the days you held me near.

Past Lovers

I used to say past lovers
had no business being friends.
What happens in this chapter
shouldn't pertain to the last.

I stand at a crossroads—
is there a middle ground to meet?
I let you in knowing
I couldn't let you leave.

I love you truly,
in all the weight of the word
in all the poems written, in all the songs sung,
in the recurring whispers when your name invades my thoughts.

I love you purely,
in all the ink my heart pumps
in all the hidden letters, in all the absent calls,
in the smiles you'll never see when I imagine you
standing next to me.

I love you fully,
in all my conviction left
in all the laughs shared, in all the tears shed
in the growing distance when my sun rises while your sun sets.

I love you
beyond how lovers should.
So let me have your presence in whatever shape it comes.
I'd rather be your friend
than be your nothing at all.

Meet me where the rooster sings

Baila, Baila, Baila,

with those words that in every swirl
dry my tears a little more.
I went out to bury my boredom
in search of new stories to write.

But there's not enough names to spark the joy yours did
nor enough tequila to help me forget
I can only find you in whiskey—a splash of James.

Hand me out a cigarette, one hit to ki(ss)(ll) my soul
and write my name into a song.
So I can live forever in different hearts
and, if lucky, meet you again in empty bars

while the rooster serenades the traffic lights
in search of new stories to tell.

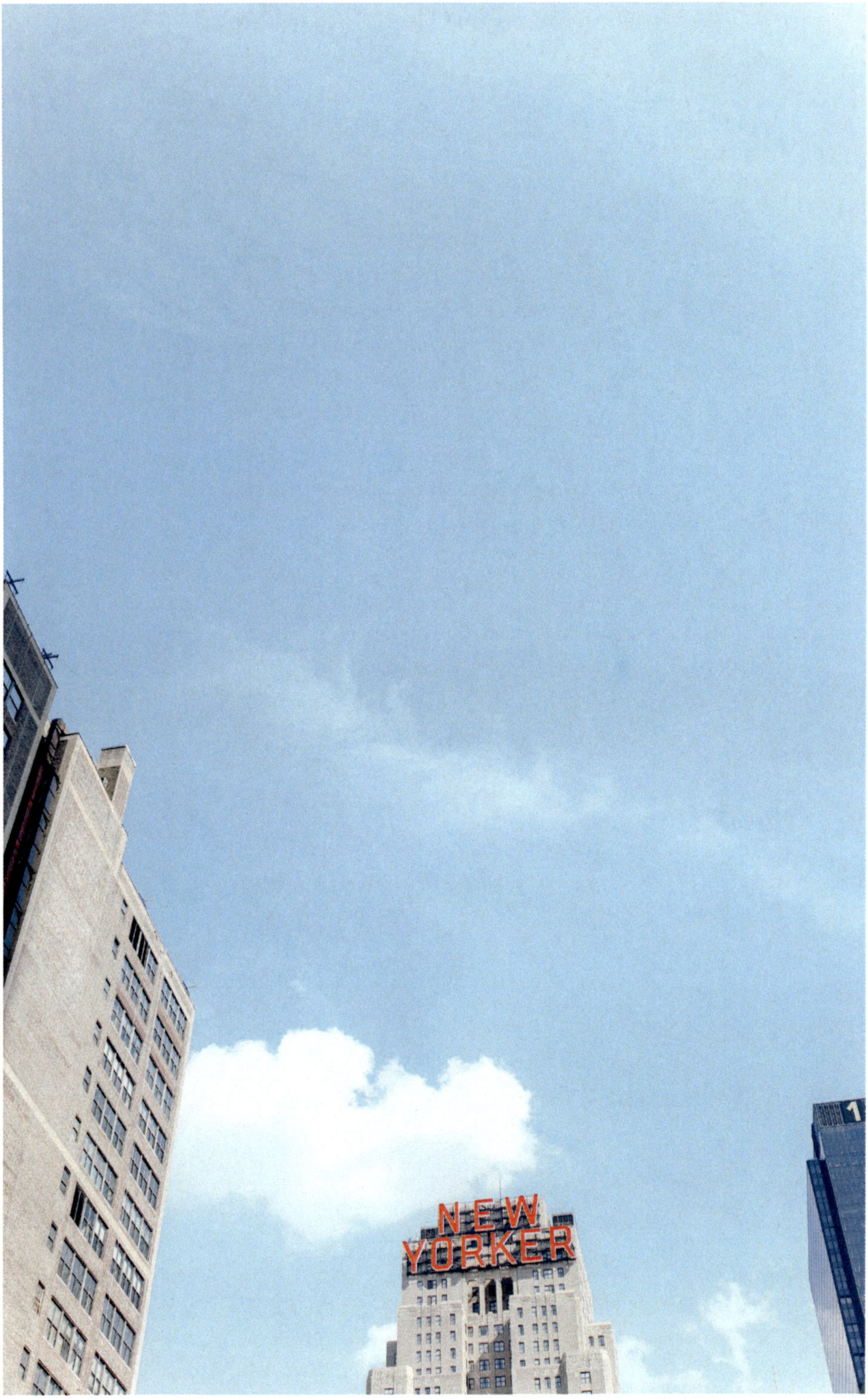
NEW
YORKER

The person I came to see and I parted ways days before we intentionally met again in New York City. We agreed that, despite our shared sentiments, our personal needs could never be met by the other in distance. I came here to enjoy the presence of happiness when sharing a bed with someone you love. To walk around the streets and become a story that will be engraved in the buildings' memories, to visit the same places together for the first time, to make a memory that will tie his story to mine, regardless of the different places, our different lives will eventually take us. I find comfort in knowing my dearest city will keep this dearest person safe, that they will be together in my absence, and in my mind; when I think of one, I'll dedicate a space of thought for the other.

The Mirror and I

What is beauty?

It's not the sunsets—
pink and violet strokes of paint
lingering before darkness overcomes them.

It's not the crashing waves—
roars of violent thunder
agonizing screams; ignorants mistake for joyful cheers.

It's not the children playing on the swings—
like adults, pretending, they're free.
Currency irrevocably strips our youth.

Beauty isn't the eternal remains of disturbed spirits.
—"Squeeze your heart and repent!" said religion.

Let your art reflect your pain
and wait to be acclaimed
for the heavenly hell you've portrayed.

Beauty is the spirit that *comes as is*—
unfit to pretend; unfit to fit
the abnormalities others deem correct.

Beauty is the spirit that rises above the sins
beneath the bone, beyond unpleasant encounters.
When all hearts close... it stays gold.

What is beauty?
Beauty is what I see
when I see you.

Checkmate

She was a queen, hunting roses from others' gardens.
Dust of dark magic descended from her touch
hexing the ghosts that once mistreated her.

She was a mother pushing lords, knights, and mad hatters away.
Always preferred to leave before being left, while her knees
bled out at night, hoping one would stay.

She was an angel sleeping in the snake's den.
Rather than sing her nature
learned to roar the displeasure of the lion, the witch, and men.

But when white flowers bloomed from the tower
the queen rested and the angel sang.
Their cuts didn't turn the roses red anymore.

—"This is what Arcadia's garden smells like," she said.

Dallas, Texas

A Postcard

The flagship of my surrenders
sails into oblivion
searching a perpetual sunset
to anchor and eternally rest
in your heart's cavity.

The walls cried
when your name wasn't sung.
The cowboys rejoiced
a lost mare returned home.

I subvert the days
we left behind
discouraged
to foreshadow a future
we get to see the sunrise
at the same time.

But New York thrives at night
he is and always will be my hardest

Goodbye.

THE END

About the Author

Mariana Lopez, a creative writer from the El Paso-Ciudad Juárez border, makes her literary debut with *His Name is New York*. Based in Dallas and working as a copywriter, Mariana weaves prose and poetry to narrate an emotional journey of love and self-discovery that mirrors the dynamic spirit of New York City. Crafted as an experience that transcends the combination of photography, prose, and poetry, it serves as a coffee table book.

She believes a book brings value to the reader's life even before it is opened.

About the Photographer

Ana Leal is a Mexican American photographer captivaed by the beauty of New York City's chaos. She focuses on documenting love in its many forms—from couples and friends to strangers on the subway.

Her passion for turning fleeting moments into lasting memories and her unwavering faith fuel her creativity.

About the Art Director

Art Director María Díaz, from Tegucigalpa, Honduras, now in Dallas, designed the captivating cover and logo for His Name is New York. Her passion for art direction emerged during her communications studies, and her award-winning work includes Graphis, Muse Creative and Creative Conscience.

Copyright © 2024 by Mariana L. Paz

All rights reserved.

No part of this publication may be reproduced in any form or by any means without the prior written permission of the publisher or author, except as permitted by U.S. copyright law. For permission requests, contact marianal.paz12@gmail.com.

Book Cover by María Díaz

Photography by Ana Leal

1st edition 2024

Made in the USA
Columbia, SC
19 November 2024

516e772a-7837-46b9-a298-c42e2e265258R01